REA

D1107959

DISCARDED

ANNEX

FREEDOM

EDUCATION

AND

THE FUND

Essays and Addresses, 1946–1956

by ROBERT M. HUTCHINS

 MERIDIAN BOOKS *New York* 1956

A Meridian Books Original Edition
First published by Meridian Books, Inc. August 1956
First printing July 1956

Copyright © 1956 by Robert M. Hutchins

Library of Congress catalog card number: 56–10021

Manufactured in the United States of America

Robert M. Hutchins

Robert M. Hutchins, President of The Fund for the Republic, began his public career as Dean of the Yale Law School and Professor of Law in 1928. At the age of thirty he became President of the University of Chicago, where his program of reform catalyzed a general reinvestigation of the foundations of humanistic education. In 1945 he became Chancellor of the University, in which position he remained until his resignation in 1951. He is the author of many works on contemporary education, among which should be noted: *No Friendly Voice, Higher Learning in America,* and *Education for Freedom.*

1205485

Acknowledgments

Mr. Arthur A. Cohen is in every way responsible for this book. He proposed it; he chose the speeches and essays that compose it; he edited them. I have been glad to accept his judgment at all points; in addition to his great natural gifts, he is better educated than I: he was graduated from The University of Chicago.

I should like, as well, to express my thanks to Kenyon College and The University of Chicago Press for permission to reprint "Morals, Religion, and Higher Education," which was delivered as the Bedell Lecture at Kenyon College in 1948. For permission to reprint, in somewhat altered form, "Democratic Dilemma," which was delivered as the Gottesman Lectures at Uppsala University in 1951, and published, with additional lectures, under the title *The Conflict in Education,* I wish to thank Harper & Brothers.

ROBERT M. HUTCHINS

Contents

Freedom, Education, and the Fund:
Essays and Addresses, 1946–1956

Introduction: FREEDOM, EDUCATION AND THE FUND

This book is either about education or about freedom; for the Fund for the Republic is an educational institution devoted to freedom. It is perhaps better to say that the book is about freedom. It does not deal with many educational questions except those in which freedom is in some way involved. Some of the essays on education are concerned exclusively with academic freedom; others try to ask what kind of educational system is appropriate to a free community or to one that wishes to be free. Even the lecture on *Morals, Religion, and Higher Education,* which on its face seems remote from the problems of freedom, is about the possibilities and limitations of education in dealing with morals and religion in a free, democratic society. The two essays on the administrator attempt to delineate the problem of democracy and efficiency in an academic setting.

Why have I chosen to speak so often about freedom? I suppose because of the tradition in which I was raised. My father's family was descended from a long line of Connecticut doctors and ministers; my mother's was a long line of sea captains from Maine. My childhood was nourished by the stories of their independence—my maternal grandfather went to sea in a sailing ship at the age of eleven and was on the voyage for four years—and I began to think at an early date that the ideal American was the perpendicular man. These ancestors of mine were all stubborn, and some of them were vain. Their notion of success did not seem to involve material goods as much as it did holding on to their own convictions in the face of external pressure. I remember that when I was about fourteen my father received for Christmas a portrait of a friend of his who had amassed a great deal of money and power by concentrating on doing so, and who looked it. My father put the photograph on the piano and said, "I will put this here to remind us of the things we are fighting against." I have sometimes thought that if I were to write my autobiography I would call it *The Picture on the Piano*.

Then there was Oberlin. My father became a professor there when I was eight, and I lived there until I went into the army at eighteen. In that stationary age Oberlin was a Puritan island in the Middle West. Nothing like it has been seen since; for the automobile and prosperity have changed the Oberlin of that day, perhaps for the better. The motto of the College was "Learning and Labor." Poverty, work, service, and what the President, Henry Churchill King, called Rational Living were the ideals that were held before us. But the principal one was non-conformity. The legacy the College left to every Oberlin man or woman of that day was the non-conformist conscience. Oberlin was the first college to admit women and the first to admit Negroes.

The great episode in the history of the College was the Wellington Raid, an occasion on which the faculty and students had gone to a neighboring town and rescued a fugitive slave. We were proud to remember that Oberlin had been a station on the Underground Railroad and to point out to one another the buildings, then still standing, that had been used for the purpose. We seriously believed that the greatest thing in the world was to lay down your life for your principles, and we considered that the Oberlin missionaries killed in the Boxer Rebellion, who were memorialized by the Martyrs' Arch in the center of the Campus, had shown us how to die.

At home and in the College I lived in an atmosphere of discussion. It was not an accident that the leading extra-curricular activity of the College was debating. There were no fraternities; their place was taken by the literary societies. We were not merely free to talk about everything; we were required to. You were entitled to your own opinion, but only if you were willing to submit it to examination and to change it if it could not survive rational scrutiny.

Neither the army, in which I conducted a successful private war against all attempts to make a soldier of me, nor Yale, then a stronghold of conformity, nor a lifetime devoted to money-raising and other forms of compromise, has been able wholly to eradicate the attitudes formed by these early influences. I still cherish the view that the independent individual is the heart of society, that his independence is his most precious attribute, and that discussion is the essence of democracy. It is hard for me to concern myself with the material prosperity of my country or with that of the individuals who compose it, because I was brought up to believe that prosperity and power were secondary, perhaps even dangerous, goals. Adjustment as the aim of education strikes me as a contradiction in terms. The Bill of Rights, instead of being a set of ancient prescriptions that do not affect me because I do not run a newspaper, do not belong to an unpopular church, and do not have to plead the Fifth Amendment, is a statement of the way in which I must demand that the Government conduct itself toward all its citizens all the time. The press appears to me as a means of purveying accurate information and as a forum for discussion, or at least as a place in which honest opinions are honestly set forth. Academic institutions are bodies of men pursuing the truth, discussing it with one another, and criticizing the environment with the utmost freedom: it is for this reason that they exist.

This, of course, is not the way things are, but the way they ought to be. I have assumed that the duty of the educator is to try to change things from the way they are to the way they ought to be. I do not assume that all or many of them can be changed. I would remind you of the words variously attributed to William the Silent and Charles the Bold: I have quoted them over and over: "It is not necessary to hope in order to undertake, nor to succeed in order to persevere."

The effort to bring about changes of the kind I have described requires a simple—perhaps too simple—faith in the rationality of man, in democracy, and in freedom. This faith leads one of the faithful to try to do what he can to develop and train the reason, to struggle for a more perfect democracy, and to fight on every front for freedom.

I became a teacher in 1921. At that time education was just escaping from the control of the classical drill-masters, who had only themselves to blame for the fate that overtook them. They claimed to train the mind, and in the revulsion against them the mind, and the training of it, lost out, too. All sorts of other ambitions came to the front, none of them defensible. A tremendous influx of students, which is scheduled to increase for the next fifteen years, overwhelmed our educational institutions after the second World War and found them without any conviction about education except that it was a good thing.

The most striking change in education in the last thirty-five years is its intellectual and moral degradation. It is hardly too much to say that the first two years of college now consist of work that was formerly done in high school. Much high school and college work is too trivial to be done anywhere; it is composed of recent inventions that are thought to have some utility in adjusting the young to their environment or in keeping them harmlessly occupied until they are old enough to go out into the world. When efforts to justify these developments have proved fruitless, their proponents have taken refuge in the allegation that large numbers have made these developments inevitable. What else can you do when you have so many students to deal with?

The moral degradation of education is evident in the current supremacy of public relations. In many colleges and universities the public relations man is either the President or the man who tells the President what to do. I concede the value of a public relations program aimed at interpreting an educational policy that has been reached and can be justified on educational grounds. I see nothing but moral degradation in an educational program that has been reached and can only be justified on public relations grounds.

The force behind public relations is the desire for money. Money appears to be a good thing in itself, without regard to the need for it or the uses to which it is to be put. Some doubt is cast on the need for it by the fact that some of the most poignant appeals for it come from some of the richest colleges and universities. A glance at any college or university catalogue will raise doubts about the uses to which money is put.

Size, numbers, quantity—in these terms we, in America, are inclined to think of all our undertakings, and it is natural that the educational system should be appraised in the same way. Numbers of students, amounts of money, the size of departments, appear both to the faculty and the public as the only intelligible criteria of success.

And so they appeared to me when I became Secretary of Yale in 1923. But I could not escape from Oberlin or from my family. I devoted myself to trying to make Yale richer and to celebrating its fame, so that it could become richer still. But my missionary past pursued me and would give me no satisfaction in my work. When I became a member of the faculty of the Law School, I thought I saw better methods of making successful lawyers than those which the School had been using. Under the tutelage of Charles E. Clark, now judge of the Circuit Court of Appeals, who was responsible for most of my legal training and for everything I did as a teacher and as Dean of the School, I learned that legal education had a long way to go toward the achievement of its announced aims. But I could not figure out why these aims were the right ones or what they had to do with the aims of a university. Why should a university help men to be successful at the Bar?

By the time I became the President of the University of Chicago, in 1929, I was full of questions; but I did not try very hard to answer them until I was forced to. That happened when the Great Depression hit us. The income of the University began to slide off so fast that our estimates had to be revised downward every day. The remedy proposed was a flat percentage reduction in our expenditures. This did not seem very intelligent to me; for anybody could see that all of our expenditures were not equally important. But what was the standard of importance? If the maintenance of buildings and grounds was not as important as the salaries of the faculty, why not? Why was the library more important than the gymnasium? It was clear that we would have to abandon a good many courses, but which ones?

My education as an administrator began when at the age of thirty-two I opened Aristotle's *Ethics* for the first time and read, "In practical matters the end is the first principle." I was shocked to realize that in the ten years I had been in universities I had never seriously asked myself what they were for. I had taken them for granted, had assumed that the aims they proclaimed were valid, and had attempted to administer them in terms of those aims. About the only idea I had of the University of Chicago when I went there was that it was great. It was my business to make it greater. The Depression seemed to postpone any immediate hope of making it greater in ways that I understood: I could not expect to make it richer; it was more likely that I would take it into bankruptcy. What was a great university, anyway?

I had to admit that the University of Chicago, and all other universities and colleges, were unintelligible to me. On the level to which I was accustomed, the level of obtaining popular support, unintelligibility seemed to me a handicap. How could the people be expected to be enthusiastic about what they could not understand? We all knew that educational institutions were not country clubs and that the records of their football teams were not an infallible index of educational excellence. But the non-educational activities of educational institutions were the ones, and perhaps the only ones, that the public could comprehend. They were almost the only ones that I could comprehend myself.

I could comprehend such non-educational activities, but I could not support them. I was trying to make education, not non-education, intelligible. The mixture of non-education with education, or what looked as though it might be education, simply confused the search for its essential character.

At about this time Charles R. Walgreen, who later became one of my closest friends, precipitated a legislative investigation of the University by charging that his niece had been exposed to subversive teachings. The investigation was a great waste of time, but it did something for me. It forced me to think about the relation of the university to the community. To think seriously about such questions demanded that not only some understanding of the good community but also of the good man be achieved. The search for an intelligible university had forced me to face fundamental questions, concerning which I had been indoctrinated at home and at Oberlin, but which I had never previously been forced to consider.

It was fortunate that, meanwhile, Mortimer Adler had dragged me, much against my will, into teaching the Great Books with him. I had read Shakespeare and Goethe, and that was about all. Plato, Aristotle, Augustine, and Aquinas, and the other books to which these led, notably those of Jacques Maritain, as well as the discussions about them that I got into with John Nef, Robert Redfield, Beardsley Ruml, Richard McKeon, Clarence Faust, and Edward Levi illuminated for me the principles I had accepted at home and at Oberlin. So did my extra-curricular activities. Talks with Scott Buchanan and Stringfellow Barr about the re-organization of St. John's College; the meetings of the Commission on the Freedom of the Press, which included Archibald MacLeish, Reinhold Niebuhr, and George Shuster, the sessions about publishing Great Books with William Benton, Alexander Meiklejohn, and Mark Van Doren; and the conferences of the Committee to Frame a World Constitution, in which many of the men I have named took part, raised the same fundamental issues.

I was a classic example of the young man brought up to good habits who could not understand why he or anybody else should have them until his own experience forced him to try to find out. Perhaps it was stubbornness or the inability to learn that led me to conclude that my early training was sound. At any rate, it seems to me that a lifetime of experience and reflection has supplied me with the reasons for defending the faith in which I was brought up.

That faith, I say again, was faith in the independent mind. Its educational consequences were belief in free inquiry and discussion. Its political consequences were belief in democracy, but only in a democracy in which the minority, even a minority of one, could continue to differ and to be heard. Those who desire to conform but are prohibited or hindered from doing so by intolerance and prejudice must be aided; the non-conformist conscience must not be stifled. Hence my interest in the Fund for the Republic.

The opportunity to establish the Fund arose because the trustees of the Ford Foundation, with which I became associated in 1951, had in the previous year announced that among its other objects the Foundation would support activities directed toward the elimination of restrictions on freedom of thought, inquiry and expression in the United States. In its early days the Foundation established several independent corporations to carry out programs that were too large and complicated for the Foundation to manage itself. W. H. Ferry, then of public relations counsel to the Foundation, and I worked out the plan for the Fund for the Republic as an independent corporation to receive funds from the Foundation for work on civil liberties. After a year and a half of discussion, the Fund was incorporated and given a sum that was expected to last about five years. When the Fund lost its President, I was glad to accept an invitation to succeed him, because the Fund combined two interests that I had had all my life; education and freedom.

I have indicated in the essay called *The Administrator Reconsidered* some of the differences between the work of a university president and that of a foundation executive. In most fields in which foundations operate, the executive can lead a sheltered life. His relationship to a large sum of money guarantees his popularity, and the objects to which the foundation is dedicated do not involve him in controversy. The Fund for the Republic, a corporation devoted to education in civil liberties, became involved in controversy merely by coming into existence. Apparently an attempt to do an honest job of showing the country what the state of civil liberties is must arouse the hostility of those who, for any reason, would prefer not to have the facts disclosed.

When I innocently accepted the Presidency of the Fund for the Republic on June 1, 1954, I made two mistakes: I overestimated the public knowledge of foundations and the way they work; and I overestimated the public knowledge of and interest in the Bill of Rights. My only excuse, in the first instance, is that nothing in my experience had prepared me for the public effects of the campaign of misrepresentation that began as soon as the program of the Fund became known. It had not occurred to me that it would be possible for hostile commentators, with simple distortion, to say that the Fund was doing something when it was clear, on the face of the record, that it was not doing it, but that one of its grantees, a highly respectable organization like a bar association or a church, was. But since foundations were mysterious and since Congressional inquiries had succeeded in creating some suspicion of them, the distortions of what the Fund for the Republic was doing were readily accepted by people who I thought should have known better.

My second mistake was misunderstanding the degree of public concern with and awareness of the Bill of Rights. For this mistake I have no excuse at all. The Chief Justice of the United States was not giving the results of any secret research when he expressed doubt as to whether the Bill of Rights could be adopted today. He was saying what everybody knows and what I forgot or chose to ignore when I began to work on the program of the Fund.

The first grant of the Fund was to the Committee of the American Bar Association on National Security and Individual Rights. That Committee decided to study Congressional investigations. Because of the ignorance of foundations to which I have referred, it was possible to convince people that, not the Bar Association, but the Fund, was studying Congressional investigations. Because of the public ignorance of and indifference to the Bill of Rights, it was further possible to make people believe that anybody who studied Congressional investigations was undermining the national security. Such a conclusion is of course irrational. My simple faith in the rationality of man compels me to regard such lapses as temporary.

One point still baffles me. A remarkable characteristic of our epoch is the use of one's attitude toward Communism and Communists as the index, touchstone, or test of one's patriotism. An enormous amount of popular, and hence effective (or it would not be popular), political argument runs this way: I am very frightened of Communism; you are not as frightened as I am; therefore, you are not as patriotic as I am. Or, in a somewhat more intelligible form: I am very much against Communism; you are not as much against it as I am; therefore, you are not as patriotic as I am. Of course, in both cases, if you are not as patriotic as I am you are not a good American. Apparently patriotism and Americanism are made proportional to one's fright of, or opposition to, Communism.

In both cases the degree of preoccupation with Communism is very important. The assumption is that, in order to show yourself properly frightened of Communism, you must think of nothing else. This appeared in the legislative inquiries into the University of Chicago, where the committees seemed to feel that unless I dropped everything and spent all my time trying to find subversive influences at work among the faculty and the students I was slightly treasonable. The fact that no charges had ever been made that any reasonable man could take seriously was irrelevant.

At a large meeting at which I spoke recently it was suggested that the address, printed in this volume, on the Bill of Rights would be much improved if it said that the Fund for the Republic was set up to fight Communism by defending and advancing the principles of the Declaration of Independence, the Constitution, and the Bill of Rights. This would mean that if there were no Communists in the world, there would be no need for the Fund, and presumably no need for the Bill of Rights when it was adopted. Admitting that Communism is most important and a most important threat to civil liberties, I believe it is still possible to say that your primary interest is in something else, like education or the general defense of civil liberties, without laying yourself open to the charge of un-Americanism.

Due process and the equal protection of the laws are the basis of our society. The Constitution provides for emergencies. The laws prohibiting espionage and subversion must be obeyed and enforced. If I insist that every person accused of crime must be given a fair trial, that accusation is not proof, and that the presumption of innocence extends to every man accused of anything, I do not expect to be called a criminal or pro-criminal or anti-anti-criminal. One would suppose that the best way to display one's Americanism would be to insist on justice under the law. To insist on it only for those who are sure to get it anyway does not seem a profitable expenditure of energy. I should have supposed that the test of one's Americanism would have been whether one was prepared to insist on justice under law for the scurviest and most unpopular persons around. They are the ones who need it. And if they don't get it, we may be certain that, if events run riot, eventually nobody will get it.

The education that should be given in our schools, colleges, and universities is that which would prepare every member of our society to play his part as a citizen of a free, democratic society. This basic education is necessary for everybody, for the suffrage is universal. But that is not the only reason. Everybody is entitled to liberal education, not only for the benefit of the community, but also for his own. The end of life is happiness. This does not mean contentment, cheerfulness, or self-satisfaction. It means, in the old phrase, activity in accordance with virtue, or the fullest development of one's highest powers. A society composed of such persons, such persons composing such a society—these are the objects of Education, Freedom, and the Fund.

April 4, 1956

PART I: *FREEDOM*

Introduction: FREEDOM

These speeches suggest a general idea of freedom and deal more specifically with political and academic freedom and the freedom of the press.

The purpose of freedom is the development of the individual and of society. Government must leave the citizen to think, to speak, to pray, and, within suitable limits, to act for himself. Discussion and criticism are indispensable to progress. At the basis of discussion and criticism lies thought. Academic groups are established for the express purpose of thinking, which involves discussion and criticism. Their claim to freedom is warranted as long as they fulfil their purpose. The freedom of the press was intended for the benefit of the people, not for the owners of the press, and rests on the people's need for information, discussion, and criticism. The freedom of the press is endangered when the press does not perform the function that is the reason for its freedom.

The first of these speeches, *The Bill of Rights: Yesterday, Today and Tomorrow,* was delivered when the Fund for the Republic was somewhat misunderstood, and was intended to explain this misunderstanding by explaining the atmosphere in which we have been living in recent years. The second, that on *Academic Freedom,* is a statement of what I take to be the classical position on academic freedom, lately reaffirmed by the

American Association of University Professors, and is designed to show that this position is correct in any atmosphere, even in, perhaps especially in, that of recent years. The primary aim of the speech, however, is to suggest that academic freedom can endure only so long as academic institutions deserve it. I cannot say that all the activities of all our academic institutions meet this requirement. The third speech is perhaps my favorite, though I admit that it was what was called a "set-up." The audience was made up of the authors of the editorials that I quoted. Out of their own mouths they had proved the charges that the Commission on the Freedom of the Press had made against them. All that was necessary was to report what they had said the Commission said and to compare it with what the Commission actually said. The fact that they allowed me to escape from the room alive is a tribute to the broad-minded tolerance of American editorial writers. Or perhaps they didn't care.

The last speech was delivered at the request of the Chairman of the Program Committee of the American Society of Newspaper Editors, who told me that he thought the time had come for the Society to have another appraisal of its performance. I mention this because I do not want anybody to think that I wander around offering gratuitous criticism to organizations in various walks of life. The main object of the speech was to indicate again the desirability of the proposal made by the Commission on the Freedom of the Press that an independent, continuing private agency be established to assess the performance of the press. Although the audience was civil in the extreme, the editorial comment around the country, which was generally to the effect that I had a sinister design to control the press, showed that publishers do not want criticism and that they will not hesitate to misrepresent suggested methods of getting it for them. This impression was confirmed in a recent poll, printed in *Editor & Publisher*, on a proposal by a committee of the journalistic fraternity, Sigma Delta Chi, to study the performance of the press in the election of 1956. A large majority of the publishers polled rejected the proposal, even though it was advanced by journalists and was to be managed by journalists. It is some consolation that the publishers of the papers generally regarded as the best were in favor of the project. But if we take the press as a whole we can only conclude that it does not care for criticism, even self-criticism.

ONE

THE BILL OF RIGHTS: YESTERDAY, TODAY AND TOMORROW

It is well known that the Bill of Rights was adopted to make certain that the individual would be protected against the government and minorities protected against the majority. It was, however, more than that, for it outlined as well the spirit and the method by which our political society was to operate. The spirit was to be that of justice and freedom. The method was to be criticism and discussion.

It was clearly unnecessary to guarantee the presentation of popular views, the practice of popular religions, or the protection of popular people. It was also unnecessary to protect the powerful against the weak. The Bill of Rights was designed to insure the defense of the weak and unpopular with respect to their persons, property, and opinions. It was not designed to save the individual from himself or to protect the government from the people. The Bill of Rights contemplates a stalwart society, where everybody thinks for himself and says what he thinks. Such a society is so confident of its strength and of the good sense of its members that it is prepared to allow anybody to say and to do almost anything.

Such a society is prepared, in the event that one of its members is accused of wrong-doing, to rely on the ancient principles of Anglo-American jurisprudence: to give the defendant the benefit of the presumption of innocence, to place the burden of proof upon his accusers, to require them to confront him in open court, to provide him with counsel, and to guarantee him a fair trial. The society contemplated by the Bill of Rights was one in which everybody could feel free, free of unjust procedures and coercive restraints.

The society envisaged by the Bill of Rights has not gone unchallenged. Having become involved in portentous international conflict, the country has witnessed the rise and increasing power of those who, either because of real fear or because they have seen political advantage in capitalizing on the fears of others, have sought to suspend or weaken the guarantees of the Bill of Rights. On occasion they have temporarily succeeded. The Bill of Rights tends to withdraw in the face of the demand for what is called "security." The delicate, but fundamental, distinctions that we have built up over the centuries between suspicion and proof, accusation and conviction, persecution and punishment, tend to become obscured. Our attitude toward government undergoes change. The basis of the Bill of Rights is that the Government is here to serve us and to help us achieve our ideals. The people exist as people to make certain, through criticism as well as voting, that it does so. Statements by the President or Congress intended to guide our thought or shape our feelings are interesting, but not decisive. The leading principle of democracy is that we are to think for ourselves. The ideal American is the perpendicular man.

When our preoccupation with what is called "security" becomes our paramount concern, our relation to the Government becomes that of the child to his nurse, or perhaps to his uncle. It is then thought that whatever the Government says we must agree with, that we must even, as in a celebrated case, be enthusiastic about it. It is natural in such circumstances that "uncooperative" can become a term of reproach indiscriminately applied to persons who stand on the Bill of Rights. It is natural that the loyalty-security system should operate even where there is no issue of security. It is natural that the Attorney-General's list of subversive organizations (about which the Attorney-General himself uttered dire warnings when he released it in 1947) should be extended far beyond the original intentions of anybody who had anything to do with bringing it into being. It is natural that few eyebrows were raised when J. Edgar Hoover said in October, 1955, that "the confidential informant has become an institution. . . ."

It is to be expected, of course, that we remain sensitive to any encroachment on the Bill of Rights when it affects ourselves or our immediate interests. Publishers, even those who have not been much interested when the Bill of Rights was invoked by other people, have insisted on the people's right to information against the government's claim that security demands secrecy. But a general apathy descends upon us in circumstances like the present. The reaction of the press to the case of Autherine Lucy was apathetic. The press did not even notice the remark of the Chairman of a House committee that there was no reason to investigate the administration of the passport regulations, because only thirteen persons had been denied the right to travel on political grounds. What is more remarkable is the apathy with which the press greeted the attack of a Senate committee on the New York *Times*.

As the Cold War lengthens, we get used to things: we don't see why the security system shouldn't be applied to second-hand piano dealers, or why anybody should feel that an anti-disloyalty oath is an impertinence, and we so far forget the presumption of innocence that when a man is accused, however irresponsibly, of Communist inclinations, we feel that if he does not immediately step forward with convincing evidence to the contrary, he admits the charge.

Discussion suffers the same fate. We become habituated to the idea that there are certain things of which we must not talk. Although the Commander-in-Chief approved, the young men of West Point and Annapolis did not debate the admission of Red China into the United Nations.

The point has been reached where even dispassionate and clearly non-political investigation of any sensitive problem is considered suspicious. When the Fund for the Republic made a grant to the Association of the Bar of the City of New York to study the loyalty-security program, the Commander of the American Legion announced that the Fund was undermining the safety of the nation.

In circumstances such as now obtain, we tend to make extensive use of meaningless name-calling. Two of the most popular names are "controversial" and "anti-anti-Communist." A man becomes controversial by being attacked. It makes little difference that the charge is shown to be frivolous and unfounded. The label sticks an unreasonably long time.

The epithet "anti-anti-Communist" is a handy device for knocking off anybody who disagrees with you. Its special value is that almost everybody can use it. Almost everybody is anti-Communist; therefore, if you are against anybody for any reason, he can say that you are anti-anti-Communist. It is depressing to see a label invented by Senator McCarthy persist after he is gone.

In the post-McCarthy atmosphere we are confronted with the paradox that, although reforms may take place, they may actually legitimize anti-libertarian principles at precisely the moment that their administration is made more lenient or rational. This is a consequence of having accepted an atmosphere of fear justified by the quest for "security."

The courts are fortunately helping us a great deal. The historic decision on desegregation, the rulings on passports, on the use of anonymous informers in a security system affecting private employment, and the decisions clarifying the use of the Fifth Amendment are evidence of the dedication of the judiciary to the Bill of Rights even in times of persistent international tension.

Anglo-American jurisprudence is a wonderful thing. But our gratitude for it and to the courts that administer it should not blind us to the fact that the problem of coping with the arbitrary exercise of governmental power is not what it used to be. The individual may now be put in the position of a defendant by any one of hundreds of agencies which may enter his life by hundreds of avenues, with dreadful consequences in the form of loss of time, effort, money, and reputation. These consequences may follow even though the individual eventually wins a clear victory. Often, as in the Peters case, the legal victory, if it is one, leaves the winner in a somewhat ambiguous position.

It is unusual to look to France for suggestions about political matters, and although British writers seldom do, some of them have lately asked whether the operations of the Conseil d'État may not be worth some study. Under the French system the citizen who regards himself as aggrieved by a governmental bureau seeks to attract the attention of the Conseil d'État. If he succeeds, he, in effect, drops out of the case as a party, and the Conseil d'État without expense to him takes over his argument with the Government. The individual watches as an interested bystander while the Government, on his behalf, tries to keep itself under control.

Mechanical devices like the Conseil d'État are easy to pass off as mere governmental machinery; yet the proper mechanics, as the history of Anglo-American procedural law teaches us, are of the first importance in the preservation of civil liberties. We must nevertheless agree that the basic matter in a democracy is public interest and understanding. If the people of this country were fully informed about and thoroughly dedicated to the Bill of Rights, appropriate machinery for carrying out their wishes would doubtless be devised. The report which Professor Stouffer of Harvard prepared for the Fund disclosed a degree of general ignorance of and indifference to the Bill of Rights that must alarm anyone concerned about the preservation of our liberties. This report confirmed the Board of Directors of the Fund in its conviction that the principal function of the Fund should be to uncover the facts about the state of civil liberties today and to promote discussion of them.

The Fund was not set up to fight Communism, but to defend and advance the principles of the Declaration of Independence, the Constitution, and the Bill of Rights. In discharging this obligation, the Fund necessarily collides with Communism, which, if it were to prevail in this country, would mean the end of the Declaration, the Constitution, and the Bill of Rights. Hence the colossal Rossiter study of the successes and failures of the Communist Party in the United States. Communism is a threat to civil liberties; and so, it may turn out, are some of the methods that we have employed to combat Communism. Hence the grants to the Association of the Bar of the City of New York to study the loyalty-security program; the study of blacklisting in the entertainment industry; the study of attempts to suppress nonconformity among teachers; the studies of censorship and of the interference of the Post Office Department with the flow of information and opinion.

Although this should give the North no grounds for complacency or self-satisfaction, it must be admitted that the principles of the Declaration of Independence, the Constitution, and the Bill of Rights are in low water in many southern states today. About a third of the commitments of the Fund for the Republic have been made, therefore, in the interracial, intergroup field. Without ignoring the problems of Mexicans, Indians, Orientals, and immigrants and aliens, the Fund has devoted the bulk of its expenditures in this area to finding out what the plight of the Negro is and promoting discussion of it, particularly in the South.

With such a program it is not to be expected that the Fund for the Republic can be universally popular. The Fund is an educational corporation. It aims at enlightenment. A good many people do not care to have light shed on dark corners that they own or occupy. A good many people do not understand that all the Fund is trying to do is to cast light. The faith of the Fund is in the common sense of the American people. As they understand that the Fund is dedicated to upholding those principles which are the essence of America, that its object is to report on the state of those principles today, and that its reports are made by the most responsible individuals and organizations that can be found, without coloration by the views of the Officers and Directors of the Fund, the criticism based on lack of knowledge will disappear, and that which is merely malicious will fall on deaf ears.

February 18, 1956   1205485

ACADEMIC FREEDOM

The arguments for academic freedom are the same as those for freedom of speech, and they rest on the same foundation. These are the familiar words of John Stuart Mill: "If all mankind minus one were of one opinion, and only one person were of the contrary opinion, mankind would be no more justified in silencing that one person, than he, if he had the power, would be justified in silencing mankind . . . The peculiar evil of silencing the expression of one opinion is, that it is robbing the human race, posterity as well as the existing generation; those who dissent from the opinion, still more than those who hold it. If the opinion is right, they are deprived of the opportunity of exchanging error for truth; if wrong, they lose, what is almost as great a benefit, the clearer perception and livelier impression of truth, produced by its collision with error."

Man is a learning animal. The state is an association the primary aim of which is the virtue and intelligence of the people. Men learn by discussion, through the clash of opinion. The best and most progressive society is that in which expression is freest. Mill said, "There ought to exist the fullest liberty of professing and discussing, as a matter of ethical conviction, any doctrine, however immoral it may be considered." The civilization we seek is the civilization of the dialogue, the civilization of the Logos.

36

In such a society the intelligent man and the good citizen are identical. The educational system does not aim at indoctrination in accepted values, but at the improvement of society through the production of the intelligent man and the good citizen. Education necessarily involves the critical examination of conflicting points of view; it cannot flourish in the absence of free inquiry and discussion.

In a democracy what the public needs to know about the teachers in the educational system is that they are competent. The competent teacher knows the subject he is teaching and how to communicate it to his pupils. Unlike the teacher in a totalitarian state, he is not supposed to purvey the prevailing dogma. He is supposed to encourage his students to use their own intelligence and to reach their own conclusions.

The definition of competence does not shift with every wind of prejudice, religious, political, racial, or economic. If competence had been the issue at Brown University during the Free Silver controversy, the President would not have been asked to resign because of his premature distaste for the Gold Standard. The modern note was struck there. What was requested of the President was "not a renunciation of his views, but a forbearance to promulgate them." And the reason was that these views were "injurious to the pecuniary interests of the University." On the other hand, the standard of competence did protect a professor at the University of Chicago who was a leading critic of Samuel Insull and the other local oligarchs of the time. He was doubtless injurious to the pecuniary interests of the University, but he and it lived through it, and he is today the senior Senator from Illinois.

We have been stifling education in this country because we have been asking the wrong questions. To ask the right questions, one asks whether or not a subject of discussion is important. Students should not be forbidden to discuss a subject, like the entry of Red China into the United Nations, on the ground that it is too important. The right question about a subject of research and the methods of investigation is whether competent scholars believe that the subject should be investigated and that this is the way to investigate it.

The Post Office Department should not be permitted to protect the Johns Hopkins School of Advanced International Studies from *Izvestia* and *Pravda*. The right question about a textbook is whether competent people think it can make a contribution to education. One does not ask whether incompetent people are going to be offended by passages taken out of context. The right question about a research man on unclassified work is whether he is competent to do it. One should not behave like the United States Public Health Service and weaken the country by withdrawing contracts from research workers on unstated grounds that can only be grounds of loyalty.

The right question about a teacher is whether he is competent. If we had been asking about competence we would have had quite a different atmosphere in the case of teachers who were Communists, or ex-Communists, who refused to testify about themselves, or declined to discuss the political affiliations of others. We have been so busy being sophisticated anti-Communists, detecting the shifts and devices of Communist infiltration, that we have failed to observe that our educational responsibility is to have a good educational system. We do not discharge that responsibility by invading civil liberties, reducing the number of qualified teachers available, eliminating good textbooks, and intimidating the teaching staff. The standard of competence means that there must be some relation between the charges against a teacher and the quality of his teaching. The standard of competence would have protected us against teachers following a party line or conducting propaganda. If a teacher sought to indoctrinate his pupils, which is the only circumstance under which he could be dangerous as a teacher, he would be incompetent, and should be removed as such. The standard of competence would have saved us from the excesses of the silly season, such as the refusal of the University of Washington to let Professor Oppenheimer lecture there on physics, and from the consequences of concentrating on the negative task of preventing one particular unpopular variety of infiltration. If we had used the standard of competence, we would have been free to fix our minds on the positive responsibility of building an educational system, and with half the energy we have put into being scared to death we might have built a great one.

Since our guilty conscience tells us that there ought to be some connection between what a man does and the punishment visited upon him, we often try to pretend that this is the rule we are following. The Attorney-General of the United States, speaking in New York during March of 1955, said that schools should not be sanctuaries or proving grounds "for subversives shaping the minds of innocent children."

This picture of subversives shaping the minds of innocent children has nothing to do with the case. The teachers who have lost their jobs in the campaign against subversives have not been charged with doing anything to the minds of any children. The case of Goldie Watson in Philadelphia is typical: testimony about the good she had done the minds of the children in her classes was rejected as impertinent. The only evidence allowed was as to whether she had declined to answer questions about her political affiliations. She had, and she was fired.

We are getting so afraid of ideas that we are afraid of people who associate with people who are said to have ideas, even if they themselves have not expressed them. The State Curriculum Commission of California is now studying investigators' reports on the authors of twenty-three textbooks. Dr. C. C. Trillingham, Los Angeles County Superintendent of Schools and a member of the Commission, said, "If an author is aligned with the Communists, we don't want his textbook, even if there is no Red propaganda in it."

We regard what a man says as irrelevant in determining whether we will listen to him. What a man does in his job is irrelevant in determining whether he should continue in it. This amounts to a decision that people whose ideas or whose associates' ideas we regard as dangerous cannot be permitted to earn a living or to make a contribution in any capacity to the well-being of the community. The Supreme Court of California has just taken this logical next step: it has held, in effect, that a Communist can have no contractual rights that the rest of us are bound to respect.

Not long ago at a dinner of the senior members of the faculty of the University of Birmingham in England, I sat across the table from a professor who is a member of the executive committee of the Communist Party of Great Britain. The British appear to be getting value out of a scholar whom none of the great American universities could appoint.

One of the more important advances in law and government effected by the struggles of our ancestors is that proclaimed by the Fifth Amendment. Why should the government demand that a man convict himself out of his own mouth instead of requiring the prosecution to make the effort to establish the charges that it has brought against him? All the Fifth Amendment means is: prove it. Injury is added to insult if there is no pretence that the questions asked must be relevant or proper. In some public school systems refusal to answer any questions by the Board of Education or any other public body is insubordination; insubordination justifies dismissal.

Surely the issue is whether the questions are legitimate. It cannot be insubordination to refuse to answer illegitimate questions. We have gone very far under the influence of one of the rollicking dicta of Mr. Justice Holmes, that there is no constitutional right to be a policeman; but not so far that public employment can be denied on a ground that has nothing to do with the duties to be performed. If the President were to refuse to employ bald-headed men in the Federal establishment, the Supreme Court would find, I believe, that the bald had been deprived of their constitutional rights.

You may say that the issue I am discussing is academic in every sense: there is no use now in talking about the right of Communists, ex-Communists, or persons who decline to answer questions about their political affiliations to teach in the United States. Milton Mayer in his recent book, *They Thought They Were Free*, tells the story of the way history passed Martin Niemoeller by. When the Nazis attacked the Communists, he was a little uneasy, but he was not a Communist, and he did nothing. When they attacked the Socialists, he was uneasy, but he was not a Socialist, and he did nothing. They went after the schools, the press, and the Jews, but he was not directly affected, and he did nothing. Then they attacked the Church. Pastor Niemoeller was a churchman. He tried to do something, but it was too late.

I hope it is not too late to point out where our preoccupation with public relations and our failure of courage and intelligence may take us. The New York *Times* on March 17, 1955 and the New York *Herald Tribune* on March 19, 1955 published editorials on the question whether teachers who decline to testify about others should be dismissed. The significant thing about the editorials is this: they both, perhaps unconsciously, extend the limits of the prevailing boycott. The *Times* condemns "adherence to Communist doctrine," thus adding theoretical Marxists to those automatically disqualified. The *Herald Tribune* comes out against Communists "or any other brands of subversives," thus opening vast new unmapped areas of investigation, recrimination, and confusion.

These two newspapers bitterly attacked the Reece Committee, appointed in the House to investigate foundations; but they appear to have succumbed to its influence, which is another evidence that if you say something outrageous authoritatively, loudly, and often enough you will eventually find yourself quoted in the most respectable places. The Reece Committee includes among the subversive almost anybody who differs with the two members of the Committee who constitute the majority. Zechariah Chafee, Jr., said at the University of Oregon in October, 1954: "The word 'subversive' has no precise definition in American law. It is as vague as 'heretical' was in the mediaeval trials which sent men to the stake." Leading the list of Reece Committee subversives are those who do not share its philosophical prejudices. The Committee condemned a philosophical doctrine, empiricism, and those who hold it, as the fountainhead of the subversive tendencies now engulfing the country. If a philosophical position can be treasonable, particularly one as harmless as a preference for fact over theory, and if two politicians can make it treasonable, freedom of thought, discussion, and teaching may not be with us long.

By repetition the Reece Committee is obtaining unconscious acceptance of another proposition, which, coupled with the proposition that politicians may declare a doctrine and its adherents subversive, still further imperils freedom of teaching and inquiry. This is the proposition that tax-exempt money is public money and that a tax-exempt institution is therefore subject to a special variety of public surveillance. An extension of this proposition is found in the California statute requiring all claimants of tax-exemption to take a non-disloyalty oath. If carried to the logical limits hinted at in the Reece Report, this notion of the public control of private, tax-exempt corporations could deprive the independent educational institutions of this country of their autonomy, that characteristic which has given them their value in the development of the American educational system.

Tax-exemption is conferred for the purpose of facilitating the performance of a public task by a private agency. A corporation that carries on education and research to that extent relieves the taxpayers of their obligation to finance such work in state-supported institutions. Tax-exemption imposes no duty on colleges and universities except that of conducting teaching and research according to their best judgment of what good teaching and research are. It does not impose the duty of making sure that the teaching and research conform to the views of the majority of a legislative committee.

Consider what those views might be. Richard E. Combs, Chief Counsel for the California Senate Committee on Un-American Activities, testified two years ago before a subcommittee of the United States Senate. He gave an account of how Communists reorient courses of instruction. He thought it worthwhile to report that the name of a course at a California university had been changed from public speaking to speech, and the books had been changed from Robert Louis Stevenson, Masefield, and Kipling to John Stuart Mill. The subversive nature of these changes may not be clear to you, but it was clear to Mr. Combs and, from all that appears, to the California committee that employs him and the committee of the United States Senate before which he testified. The appraisal of courses of study or of the performance of teachers is a professional job, not to be undertaken by the naive and unskilled.

Consider the role of the California Senate Committee on

Un-American Activities in the administration of California institutions of higher learning. The Committee claims that a chain of security officers on campuses has been welded by its efforts. If its claims are correct, and they have been disputed, professors and students at eleven institutions are being continuously spied upon for the benefit of a legislative committee. The Committee has an arrangement whereby it passes on the qualifications of members and prospective members of the faculties from the standpoint of their Americanism. The reason for this is said to be that the colleges and universities are not competent to assess the Americanism of their teachers, and the Committee is. According to the Committee at least one hundred members of these faculties have been forced to resign and at least one hundred prospective members have failed of appointment because of the Committee's work. It is too bad that the Committee has not disclosed the information that led to the interdiction of its victims. One shudders to think that it may have been enough to have been heard quoting John Stuart Mill.

But the issue of legal control is not basic. Academic freedom comes and goes because of some conviction about the purpose of education on the part of those who make the decisions in society. The Kaiser gave professors freedom of research because he believed that this was one way to make Germany strong and prosperous. This freedom did not extend to professors who wanted to engage actively in politics on the wrong side, the side of the Social Democratic Party. The Kaiser did not set a high value on independent criticism.

In a democratic community the question is: what do the people think education is and what do they think it is for? I once asked a former Minister of Education of the Netherlands what would have happened if he had exercised his undoubted legal authority and appointed professors of whom the faculties of the Dutch universities did not approve. He said, "My government would have fallen." He meant that the people of Holland would not tolerate political interference with the universities: they understood the universities well enough to recognize interference when they saw it and felt strongly enough about it to make their wishes effective.

The public officers and businessmen who are the trustees of the provincial universities in the United Kingdom have legal control over them, but would never think of exercising it in any matter affecting education and research. They limit themselves to business. The tax-payers now meet more than half the cost of Oxford and Cambridge, but no Englishman supposes that this entitles the government to exert any influence in their academic affairs.

If the people believe that independent thought and criticism are essential to the progress of society, if they think that universities are centers of such criticism and that the rest of the educational system is intended primarily to prepare the citizen to think for himself, then academic freedom will not be a problem, it will be a fact. Under these circumstances teachers would not be second-class citizens subject to limitations of expression and behavior that show the public thinks the teacher of today is the nursemaid of yesterday. A teacher would be appointed because he was capable of independent thought and criticism and because he could help the rising generation learn to think for itself. He would be removed only if those who appointed him proved to be mistaken in these matters. The proof of their error would have to be made to persons who could understand the issue—an out-of-hand administrative removal approved by a board of laymen without participation by academic experts is a denial of academic freedom.

The people of this country think that education is a perfectly splendid thing and have not the faintest idea of what it is about. The reason that they are in this condition is that educators have had no time and little inclination to explain. After all, the great desideratum of American education in the last thirty-five years has been money. If you want money, you do not talk about independent thought and criticism; you do not engage in it too obtrusively; you may even suppress it if it becomes too flagrant. To get money you must be popular. "He thinks too much" is a classical reference to an unpopular man. Or as a great industrialist once remarked to a friend of mine, "You are either a Communist or a thinker."

I have no doubt that much of the trouble of recent years

about academic freedom has been the result of the Cold War and our panic about it. As Professor Chafee has said, "Freedom of speech belongs to a people which is free from fear." But the basic issue is public understanding. If public understanding were serious and complete, the Cold War could not have thrown us off our balance.

I do not deny that many eloquent statements of the purpose of American education have been made. They cannot offset the impression created by the official propaganda of educational institutions, by their fatuous efforts to please everybody, and by their emphasis on the non-intellectual and even anti-intellectual activities associated with education in this country. Freedom of teaching and research will not survive unless the people understand why it should. They will not understand if there is no relation between the freedom that is claimed and the purpose it is supposed to serve. If the teacher of today is the nursemaid of yesterday, he does not need academic freedom—at least the nursemaid never did.

Academic freedom is indispensable to the high calling of the academic profession. If the profession is true to the calling, it will deserve the freedom, and it will get it.

April 2, 1955

THREE

FREEDOM AND THE RESPONSIBILITY
OF THE PRESS: 1948

Since some members of the National Conference of Editorial
Writers apparently could not grasp the import of the Report
of the Commission on the Freedom of the Press because our
style was dense and dark, I shall try to express what I think of
you in words both few and short, hoping thereby that lucidity
will result.

I shall begin by paying you the greatest compliment in my
power. I think you are teachers. I do not say you are good
teachers: witness your response to the Report of the Commission on the Freedom of the Press. By this test the New York
Herald Tribune, the Washington *Post,* the Washington *Star,*
the *Christian Science Monitor,* and the St. Louis *Star-Times*
are good teachers. But a good teacher has to know how to read.
Not all newspaper editors know how. The Report said, "The
Commission does not believe that it (the press) should be
regulated by government like other businesses affected with a
public interest, such as railroads and telephone companies."
The Columbus *State Journal* reacted to the Report, however,
by commenting: "The most fallacious premise of all is that
the press, to protect itself from its own shortcomings, should
submit to the type of governmental regulation meted out to
public utilities."

The Commission said it saw no hope in self-regulation. The St. Louis *Post-Dispatch* and the Los Angeles *Times* said they could not be for the Commission because it was for self-regulation.

A good teacher has to try to be fair. He cannot use the straw man or the red herring. The New York *Times,* in the midst of a most kind editorial, sought to answer the Report by saying that there was no sign of a general conspiracy to suppress or distort facts on the part of the owners and managers of the press. This is the straw man. The Commission did not even hint at conspiracy. What it said was that "The owners and managers of the press determine which persons, which facts, which versions of facts and which ideas shall reach the public." If this is true, it is important; a conspiracy is not required to make it either true or important.

And how am I to understand the statement of my old and dear friend Nat Howard, who, with the aid of the Louisville *Times,* notes that the Commission spent $215,000, "the detailed disbursement of which has not been made public." I am not much consoled by the remark of the Louisville *Times,* "There was not a shadow or suspicion of misdoing."

By putting the headline "Professors and Freedom" on its editorial the *Wall Street Journal* could prove, as did the Shreveport *Times,* that the Commission was Red, though the Chairman of the Federal Reserve Bank of New York and the General Counsel of the Pennsylvania Railroad were among its members. The *Wall Street Journal* quotes the Commission: "We recommend the repeal of legislation prohibiting expressions in favor of revolutionary changes in our institutions where there is no clear and present danger that violence will result from the expression." A good teacher ought to know what he is talking about. The *Wall Street Journal* ought to know that such laws have been held unconstitutional and that the aim of the Commission was to wipe the rest of them off the books, so that a man would not have to take his case to the Supreme Court to prove that he was imprisoned unconstitutionally. One reason why the *Wall Street Journal* ought to know this is that the Commission says so in so many words.

And how would you like to have your child taught by *The*

Knickerbocker News? The headline of its editorial is: "Professors Blindly Try to Curb Press by Regulations to End All Our Liberties." The editorial says that the Commission advocated the correction of the alleged defects of the press by government regulation. This is a lie. It says that I am young. This is a lie. It says that ten of the thirteen members are professors. This does not prove that they are liars. It says that the Report was a criticism of other media by one publishing group, that of Mr. Luce, and that it was made for Mr. Luce's profit. This is a laugh. But I will let *The Knickerbocker News* do its own name-calling, and leave it with you. It says, "Finally, the charge that the press generally excludes worthy news in favor of sensationalism is a downright lie that would disgrace the lips of an idiot."

The big red herring, or bloater, was, of course, the fact that many members of the Commission were professors and that none was, at the date of writing the Report, a member of the press. The Shreveport *Journal,* the San Antonio *Express,* the Columbus *Dispatch,* the Troy *Morning Record,* and Mr. John H. Crider in the Boston *Herald* thought that by tossing their readers this fish for breakfast or for tea, as the case might be, they would divert them from the Commission's criticisms. But was the fact that many commissioners were professors really important? I should have thought not. A teacher who was trying to be fair would have told his pupils that Chafee was the leading authority on freedom of expression in the United States, that Clark was the leading economist, that Hocking was the dean of philosophers, that Lasswell was one of the leading students of communication, that Merriam was the dean of political scientists, that Niebuhr was the leading theologian, that Redfield was one of the leading students of culture, that Schlesinger was the leading American historian, and that Dickinson, in addition to being General Counsel for the Pennsylvania Railroad, was one of the leading political scientists and constitutional lawyers of our time.

Do you suppose that, if a commission to study academic freedom were composed largely of such men as Charles Merz, and Geoffrey Parsons, and Savellon Brown, and Ernest Kirschten, and John Crider, and Nat Howard, and Barry Bingham, and Erwin Canham, any teacher who pretended to be good would have the nerve to tell the public that their report could be disregarded because they were a bunch of newspapermen who didn't know anything about education? Do newspaper writers believe that their business is so esoteric that intelligent laymen who have consumed their product all their lives can have nothing to tell them that is worth listening to? I think the recent President's Commission on Higher Education failed because so many of its members were educators; all we learned from them was that they wanted twice the money they were getting. This, or something like this, is what one is likely to hear when the vested interests tell the public about themselves. The Commission on the Freedom of the Press was set up to tell the truth about the press. Where we needed information, we asked the members of the press to give it to us. I would like to have a lay commission tell the truth about higher education in the United States, and I would like to have it go about it in the same way.

There was, among previously mentioned complaints, the allegation that the Commission produced no new facts. Many of the papers I have referred to mentioned this damaging point, and the Dallas *Morning News* made it the theme of its editorial. The man who wrote the editorial for the *Examiner* of Independence, Missouri, a man who can neither read nor write, said: "We fail to find anything in this report we did not know and appreciate and criticize ourselves and we refuse to accept the idea that the whole newspaper press is venal and controlled because there are such papers and we know there are such papers." I take it that the real question about the Report is whether it is true. If it is true, then the fact, if it is a fact, that it is not new makes it all the worse. If the facts have been known and yet nothing has been done about them, the press is twice guilty. In words both few and short, as promised, the press is guilty of inveteracy and recidivism.

The Report, moreover, did not come from professional agitators against the press. If the names and training of the members of the Commission are important at all, they are important in this: charges, many of which had been shrugged off as the muckraking of professional agitators, were now confirmed by the serious study of sober men. The Commission stated, and it was obvious from its composition anyway, that its object was to think about the press and its freedom, with a view to improving the one and saving the other. It was not trying to dig up new dirt. The Commission was appointed to explore the realm of principles and ideas, not the realm of facts. An explorer in the realm of principles and ideas has to have his facts straight; but to condemn him for failing to discover *new* facts is like condemning Einstein because he is not Admiral Byrd.

In a different vein, the Chicago *Times,* the Springfield *Union,* and the New York *Daily News* certainly must have been joking when they told their readers that the press was not in need of criticism because the great American public criticizes it every day by simply failing to buy the paper if it doesn't like it. The inference is that the press must be doing right by its readers or else it wouldn't have so many.

Such a view must be ironic for the citizens of Kansas City, Minneapolis, Springfield, Worcester, Rochester, Trenton, Toledo, Omaha, Des Moines, Richmond, Louisville, and Galveston, to name only a few, where people have to buy the papers of one owner or go without. What a consolation the privilege not to buy must be to the people of Arizona, Delaware, Minnesota, Montana, New Hampshire, North Dakota, South Carolina, Virginia, and Wyoming, where, according to Senator Murray's report to a Senate Committee, there are no locally competing daily newspapers whatever. Moreover, even if there are competing local papers, and they are essentially alike, the reader still has no real choice. The argument that the press must be good or it wouldn't have readers is, under these circumstances, like telling the disgusted radio listener that he can turn to three other stations and hear commercials and programs just as bad as the ones he has been listening to.

The fact that more people are in schools, colleges, and universities today than ever before does not prove that the people like the schools, colleges and universities. It proves that more people want education today than ever before, and that in order to get some they will take what the schools, colleges, and universities have to offer. If all schools, colleges, and universities are substantially alike, the people have no choice. And if there is one school, or college, or university in a region, it would hardly do to say that large attendance from the region showed that it was good.

It is neither logically nor practically true that the university with the largest attendance is necessarily the best. This applies equally to the newspaper. A university and a newspaper must both command popular support in order to survive. But a university and a newspaper, or any other organization or corporation, must be judged in terms of its purpose. If the purpose of a university is to have a lot of students, then the university that has the most is the best. If the purpose of a newspaper is to make a lot of money, then the newspaper that makes the most is the best. If, however, the purpose of universities and newspapers is the same, to the extent that both should aim at public enlightenment, largeness and profit become irrelevant.

It is possible that in fulfilling its enlightening responsibility, a university or a newspaper may have to offer its constituency instruction that is unpalatable to the members of that constituency. I presume the press by and large agrees with this, since for some sixteen years newspapers in the United States have been urging their readers to vote for candidates whom they did not want and would not elect. Notwithstanding, a great deal of time is spent blaming the tone of the press on the people, and saying that the public is only being given what it wants. One must conclude by the contradiction of your behavior and your pretension that you are disingenuous in claiming that you have to give the public what it wants. This argument college presidents employ to justify intercollegiate football. We all employ this argument to justify practices that we are too wicked or too lazy to abandon. If the press really meant it, it would have been among the most ancient supporters of Roosevelt and Truman. I conclude that it does not really mean it.

If the press wishes to repudiate the Report and silence me, it can attack my major premise. It may deny that its function is to teach. If, however, newspaper editors and writers are not teachers, what are they? They are either entertainers or the hired hands and voices of men who happen to have enough money to own newspapers. In neither case would they have any serious claim to public attention.

I hasten to say that I have great respect for men who have money; I wish I knew more of them more intimately. But as we have passed the time when a single man could by virtue of his money make a university the reflection of his whims and fancies, so I wonder whether we may not some day come to the point when a single man cannot by virtue of his ownership make a large metropolitan daily the reflection of his whims and fancies, limited only by the willingness of the public to continue to pay him to learn what his current whims and fancies are.

The Commission on the Freedom of the Press took the position that the newspaper business was and should remain a private business, and to that position I adhere. But there are some interesting experiments that might be tried within the realm of private business. For example, the Washington *Post*, the London *Times*, and the London *Economist* now have trustees, who are well-known public figures, who must approve the transfer of any shares of stock; and in the case of the *Economist* the trustees must appoint, or, if necessary, dismiss the editor and must be unanimous in doing so.

Under arrangements like this or perhaps under better arrangements that could be worked out, editorials would not necessarily reflect the political, economic, and social views of the owner. They would represent his interest in public enlightenment. He would offer them not because they were his, or even because he agreed with them, but because they were worth listening to. The device of the signed editorial could be used to make clear that the writer did not represent the owner in any other sense than this.

The sole test of the success of a steel business or a cracker business may be, for all I care, its ability to make money; but the public concern with the large elements in the newspaper business suggests that, though a newspaper must make money to stay in business, it should meet a further test; it is proper to ask whether it is discharging its responsibility for public enlightenment.

The balance sheet of a newspaper does not help in answering this question much more than a university's does. The fact that a newspaper has made its owner rich does not automatically lead to the conclusion that he must be a good educator, or even a good newspaperman. Hence I agree with the Washington *Post* that probably the most important recommendation of the Commission on the Freedom of the Press is that which proposes the creation of a new, independent, continuing agency to appraise the performance of the press in discharging its responsibility for public enlightenment. Cherished among my souvenirs is the remark of the Lynchburg *News* that men who were willing to accept membership in such an agency would show by that fact alone that they were not qualified for the work. I can only assume that the Lynchburg *News* thinks that if a man is willing to perform a public service he must be disqualified for it. On this theory Washington, Lincoln, and Senator Glass would all have been excluded from public life.

If the newspaper business is to continue to be a private business, a newspaper must continue to be under the control of its owner. If the owner is irresponsible, the paper must be so. How can the owner be made responsible? Those who hold the legal title to universities have been made as responsible as they are through a campaign that began a thousand years ago and that continues to this day. This campaign has been conducted to instruct those within and those without the profession as to the purposes of educational institutions and the status that teachers must have in order to discharge their responsibilities. This campaign has laid the foundations of the legal rights that professors enjoy, and, what is far more important, it has developed the tradition within which they operate. The fact that the tradition is more important than the legal arrangements is evidenced by the academic freedom that in some places has been guaranteed to professors even when they are on annual rather than life appointments. The tradition seems to be the cause of the contractual arrangements, rather than the other way round. It seems likely that good teaching would be impossible without this tradition, which is designed to protect the teacher against domination by any boss inside his institution or by any pressure group outside it. This tradition enables him to use such intelligence as he has for the enlightenment of the public. I am very far from saying that we have much good teaching in this country; I do say we should not have as much as we have without this tradition, and that perhaps the chief reason why we have not more is that this tradition is even yet imperfectly understood and established.

If, then, you, as editors and newspaper writers, are teachers, and if good teaching requires some such tradition, and perhaps contractual arrangements reflecting it, how can we take some few steps toward it in our lifetime? One thing that would be helpful would be to have you stop exhibiting neurotic symptoms every time anybody criticizes you. After all, your right to criticize is protected by a constitutional provision. But I never understood that the First Amendment said that the right of the press to be free from criticism is forever guaranteed; or that anybody who criticizes the press should be regarded as seeking to repeal this amendment. The press is the only uncriticized power in the country. You criticize everybody else, but if anybody criticizes you, you respond in the way you responded to the Report of the Commission on the Freedom of the Press. Such response suppresses criticism. The result of such response can only be that intelligent people who have something useful to do will no longer waste their time trying to help you out. Why should they, when their reward is indifference, misrepresentation, and intimidation?

The tradition of freedom and independence that good teaching requires cannot be built without criticism of the existing practices of the press. The editorial writers ought to be plugging every day for the independent, critical agency recommended by the Commission on the Freedom of the Press. You ought to demand that it be created. You ought to insist that the money be raised for it. You ought to build it up as one of the most important and pressing projects in American life, so that no man of public spirit could decline to serve on it. You ought to point out that, through such an agency, the principles by which the press can remain a private business and perform a public service without governmental regulation may be worked out and made effective. You ought to emphasize that, through such an agency, the relations between you and the owners of your papers may be put on such a basis that you can have the freedom and independence you need to perform your teaching task. You ought to keep repeating that through such an agency the standards of public service, which must supplement, if they do not replace, the balance-sheet standard, might eventually be developed. You ought to make clear that you now perform your teaching function subject to the hazards of the balance sheet and the much more serious hazards of the personal tastes and prejudices of those who own, and own in a very literal sense, the educational institutions to which you belong. The hazards of the balance sheet exist, more or less, for any teacher; the additional hazards to which you are subjected are too much. If the present owner of any paper is a good newspaperman and a good educator, what assurance is there that his successor will be? The Commission on the Freedom of the Press sought to show the public the kind of freedom and independence you require.

No one will deny that the world is in a terrible state. No one will deny that the American press is potentially a tremendous instrument of public enlightenment. No one will deny that the American people need all the light they can get. In the present crisis the people should be eagerly looking to the press for guidance. I do not need to tell you that they are not doing so. They may be buying the papers; but they are paying no attention to the advice they give. This is unfortunate; for the advice of the press may be right. It is unfortunate, also, because it means that at a time when we need all the light we can get, a tremendous instrument of public enlightenment is not shedding much effective illumination.

What causes this? The reason the people who buy newspapers do not take their advice is because they do not believe what they say. They do not believe what you say because they do not believe you are disinterested. They do not believe you are responsible. They will not accept you as teachers because they know that editorial writers do not operate within the tradition that is necessary for good teaching. They may buy the papers for countless reasons: to find out what has happened to Dagwood, or who won the fifth race at Santa Anita, or what is on sale at Gimbel's. They do not buy them for the editorials. They read the editorials, if at all, for amusement; they do not read them for instruction. Yet I think you are teachers. If you are to have pupils, public confidence in you must be established.

November 19, 1948

FOUR

FREEDOM AND THE RESPONSIBILITY OF THE PRESS: 1955

In 1930, some twenty-five years ago, I last had the honor of confronting the American Society of Newspaper Editors. The quarter of a century between has been the longest in history. That was a different world, before the Depression, before the New Deal, before the Newspaper Guild, before the suburbs, before they charged for newsprint, before the atom, before television. It was a world in which the press was powerful and numerous. Though the press is powerful still, some eight hundred papers that were alive then are gone now. Twenty-five years hence, when I am eighty-one, where will the press be?

When last here, I said: "The greatest aggregation of educational foundations is the press itself . . . Indeed I notice that in spite of the frightful lies you have printed about me I still believe everything you print about other people . . . If the American press does not need or cannot get the leadership of some endowed newspapers, we must fall back on the long process of education through educational institutions, hoping that in the long run we may produce a generation that will demand better things of you. This process will be tedious and difficult, because of the power of the press itself over the minds and habits of those whom the educational institutions produce."

Though I am neither prophet nor preacher, my words were not attended. I would merely remind you that a great many men who paid no attention then are not here now.

I joined in another effort in your behalf in 1947, when the Report of the Commission on the Freedom of the Press appeared. The Commission felt a little sad. It said, "The outstanding fact about the communications industry today is that the number of its units has declined." It expressed a high opinion of your role in life, for it said, "Freedom of speech and freedom of the press are moral rights which the state must not infringe." And again, "We must recognize that the agencies of mass communication are an educational instrument, perhaps the most powerful there is."

You were furious. Your president issued a statement in six paragraphs, in three of which he said that the members of the Commission were "left-wing," and in all of which he stated his conviction that, since most of the members of the Commission were professors without experience in the newspaper business, nothing they said could be of any importance, although it might be dangerous. At the meeting of this society in 1947, to which I had expected to be invited to receive your congratulations, the only thing that saved me from condemnation was the expressed unwillingness of your committee to "dignify" me by such action.

All over the country you attacked the Report. I hope you will read it sometime. But for fear you won't, I shall quote a passage from it that will give you the main idea: "If modern society requires great agencies of mass communication, if these concentrations become so powerful that they are a threat to democracy, if democracy cannot solve the problem simply by breaking them up—then those agencies must control themselves or be controlled by government. If they are controlled by government, we lose our chief safeguard against totalitarianism—and at the same time take a long step toward it."

A kind of neurotic sensitivity is characteristic of the press throughout the English-speaking world. The British papers were outraged by the report of the Royal Commission on the Press, which was almost as mild as ours. I don't know what makes the press feel this way. After all, in this country there is a special amendment to the Constitution, and the first one at that, protecting it. Perhaps it is this special dignity that sometimes leads newspapers to confuse their private interests with those of the public. One of the most celebrated managing editors in the country told our Commission that the only threat to the freedom of the press was the Newspaper Guild and that all we had to do was to adopt a resolution denouncing the Guild and go home. Most papers saw Marshall Field's suit against the AP as the end of freedom of the press. All he wanted to do to the AP was to join it. About once a week you break out in exasperation against anybody who tries to keep anything from you, for reasons of state or for any reason at all. You are the only uncriticized institution in the country. You will not criticize one another, and any suggestion that anybody else might do so sets you to muttering about the First Amendment.

I know that lately life has been hard for you. And it may get even worse; for it may turn out that reading is an anachronism. When I was a boy, reading was the only established and available path to knowledge, information, or even entertainment. But the other day in Hollywood I met a man who was putting the Great Books on records. Everything else has already been put on records or films. One glance at the children making for the television set on their return from school is enough to show that this is a different world. The habit of reading, which my generation fell into because there was not much else to do, may now not be formed at all; it may have too much competition.

The competition may win. Gresham's Law of Culture is that easy stuff drives out hard. It is harder to read, even after Dr. Flesch has finished with the printed page, than it is to look and listen. I do not believe that newspapers can do what comic books, picture magazines, motion pictures, and television can do in glorious technicolor. Since they can do this kind of thing better, why should you do it at all?

You may say it is the only way to survive. John Cowles suggests it may be a way to die. In his Sigma Delta Chi speech he said newspapers have realized that complete and fair coverage builds circulation. With few exceptions, he said, those newspapers which "have had the heaviest circulation losses are not papers that regard full and fair news presentation as their primary function and reason for existence." If so good a businessman as Mr. Cowles can think there is *any* chance that sensationalism and entertainment are not good for business, a layman may perhaps be forgiven for being impressed.

Emboldened by his example, I will say that newspapers should do as well as they can the things that they can do best, and they should leave to others the responsibility of entertaining the public. If you are worried about who is going to discharge that responsibility, read the March 21, 1955 issue of *Newsweek*, which says that television is abandoning "Johns Hopkins Science Review," "Princeton, '55," and "The Search." These programs have won many honors and audiences that look large to people who do not work in advertising agencies.

A couple of years ago Henry Luce was discussing the monopoly newspaper. He said the argument against it was that it deprived the community of differing presentations of news and opinions. He went on, "Like so many high-brow discussions about newspapers (I notice that journalists invariably use the word 'high-brow' when referring to criticisms of the press, even when, as in this case, the truth of the criticism is self-evident to the merest moron) this one is fine, except that it ignores the actual nature of a newspaper. Does any one feel strongly that a city ought to have several newspapers in order to offer the community a greater variety of comic strips, breakfast menus, and cheesecake?" If this is the actual nature of a newspaper, the fewer papers the better. Certainly the special constitutional protection thrown about them seems no more warranted than such protection would be for acrobats, chefs, beauty parlor operators, and astrologers.

What the framers of the First Amendment had in mind was debate, a great continuing debate, with the people hearing all sides and getting all the facts. If government could be kept from interfering with this debate, nothing could interfere with it; for a man who differed with the existing papers could start one of his own. The Founding Fathers did not foresee that 94 per cent of American cities and eighteen American states would be without competing papers. In the overwhelming majority of communities there can now be no debate among rival editors. The editor in a one-paper town has the only voice there is, and the only one there is likely to be. The debate has become a soliloquy.

Talk about the virtues of monopoly is the flimsiest rationalization, as is shown by the poor quality of the papers in many monopoly towns. Monopoly cannot be a good thing. At its best it can be like a benevolent despotism, good while the benevolence lasts, but an accident in any case. Monopoly may in the present state of affairs be a necessary evil, but let us not pretend that it is not an evil.

Rising costs have put the publisher in the driver's seat, where he has no business to be. The First Amendment was not instituted to give a preferred position to people who were making money out of papers as against those who were making money out of other articles of commerce. The Amendment was to protect the content of the press, not the cash return from it. The reason the publisher is in the driver's seat is that it costs so much money to own and operate a newspaper, and more all the time. If the soliloquy is that of one of the richest men in town, it is more than likely that it will sound the same political note as other soliloquies in other towns, rendered by other rich men. This is the basis of the phrase, "a one-party press."

Of course we have a one-party press in this country, and we shall have one as long as the press is big business, and as long as people with money continue to feel safer on the Republican side. For sheer psalm-singing sanctimoniousness no statement in recent years has surpassed that of Charles F. McCahill, president of the American Newspaper Publishers Association, when he was asked to comment on Adlai Stevenson's polite remarks on a one-party press. Mr. McCahill said, and I quote him: "It is the responsibility of the individual editor and publisher to decide what is printed in a particular newspaper. Fortunately, there is no power in this country to standardize the editorial views of any editor or publisher." Here in two sentences Mr. McCahill managed (1) to say what everybody knew already; (2) to be completely irrelevant; and (3) to prove Mr. Stevenson's point for him by making the partisan insinuation that Mr. Stevenson wanted the power to standardize editorial opinion. How you get along with these publishers is more than I can understand.

Lord Beaverbrook, when he was asked by the Royal Commission on the Press what his purpose in life was, replied under oath: "I run the paper purely for the purpose of making propaganda, and with no other motive." (There is apparently less cant among publishers in England than we are accustomed to here.) Lord Beaverbrook's propaganda collides wherever it goes with the counter-propaganda of numerous local and national voices. The popular press in Britain is the most sensational in the world, but an Englishman who doesn't want a sensational newspaper does not have to take the *Mirror*. Because of the geography of England he can get anywhere, inexpensively, and usually with his breakfast, a presentation of the news as fair as an editor can make it and as full as the restrictions on newsprint will allow, together with serious commentary upon it.

In the absence of some new technological revolution the number of papers per community in this country seems unlikely to increase. Nothing suggests that costs will fall. Television and suburbanization are driving ahead as fast as they can go. As monopoly continues to spread, the ancient check of competition can of course no longer be relied on.

This should lead to the burial of that consoling reference to Jefferson's Second Inaugural, an ever-present refuge in time of criticism, which made its last formal appearance in the statement of your committee commenting on the Report of the Commission on the Freedom of the Press. Jefferson said, in effect, that the people would make their views of a newspaper felt by refusing to read, believe, or buy it. The theory that the daily test of the market place is an expression of public criticism, and all that is needed, is reduced to absurdity when the public has no option, when it has to buy the newspaper that is offered or go without.

If we cannot look to competition to keep publishers from getting out of hand, what can we do to save their freedom from the consequences of their irresponsibility? My youthful suggestion of some endowed newspapers was designed to ex-

ecute some publishers *pour encourager les autres.* The object
was to set some standards that publishers of unendowed newspapers might be held to. I take this proposal less seriously than
I did twenty-five years ago. The *Christian Science Monitor*
undoubtedly has a good influence on the press of this country,
but the conditions under which it operates, with its foundations in heaven rather than on earth, are so different from the
ordinary that any publisher has an adequate excuse for not following the *Monitor's* example. So I fear it would be with an
endowed newspaper.

A trust such as that which controls the future of the Washington *Post* regulates the selection of stockholders, but gives
the editor no explicit protection. The British trusts usually
have the same object, that of preventing the ownership from
falling into unsuitable hands. Although the British trusts reflect an attitude that an editor would find reassuring, no trust
covering a daily newspaper leaves him formally any better off
than he would be if there were no trust. The most that the
Royal Commission was willing to say was, "A trust does not
necessarily convert a newspaper from a commercial to a non-
commercial concern or give it quality which it did not possess
. . . A trust can be, however, a valuable means of preserving
quality where quality already exists. We accordingly welcome
the action of public-spirited proprietors who have taken such
steps as lie in their power to safeguard the character and independence of their papers; and we hope that the number of papers so protected will grow."

A publisher's willingness to establish a trust shows that he
could be trusted without it; still it is a way of extending the
benevolence of the benevolent despot beyond the limits of his
own life. When you have a newspaper worth protecting, a
trust will help you protect it; but a trust does not guarantee
you a newspaper worth protecting.

The purpose of a newspaper, and the justification for the
privileges of the press, is the enlightenment of the people
about their current affairs. No other medium of communication can compete with the newspaper in the performance of
this task. A newspaper that is doing this job well is a good
newspaper, no matter how deficient it may be in astrology,

monus, comics, cheesecake, crime, and Republican propaganda. A newspaper that is doing this job deserves protection against government, and it will certainly need it.

A newspaper that is doing this job will have to bring before its readers points of view with which it disagrees and facts that it deplores. Otherwise in monopoly towns the people cannot expect to be enlightened; for television and radio are unlikely to be in the same class with a well-run newspaper in telling what is happening and what it means. Television and radio are, moreover, controlled by a governmental agency, and one that does not inspire much confidence today.

A good many newspapers take seriously their responsibility to enlighten the people about current affairs. It is generally agreed that the best American papers are as good as any in the world and that the average is high. Our question is how to maintain the good newspapers in the faith and how to convert the others.

I think the opposition to the principal recommendation of the Commission on the Freedom of the Press ought to be reconsidered. This recommendation was that a new agency be established to appraise and report annually upon the performance of the press. The Commission said, "It seems to us clear that some agency which reflects the ambitions of the American people for its press should exist for the purpose of comparing the accomplishments of the press with the aspirations which the people have for it. Such an agency would also educate the people as to the aspirations which they ought to have for the press." The Commission suggested that this agency be independent of government and of the press; that it be created by gifts; and that it be given a ten-year trial, at the end of which an audit of its achievement could determine anew the institutional form best adapted to its purposes. The fact that the British commission independently reached an identical recommendation seems to me highly significant.

Such an agency should contain representatives of the press; it should also contain laymen. My guess is that the weakness of the Press Council in Sweden results from the fact that it is composed entirely of representatives of the newspapers. I believe that the British Council will go the same way because the press rejected the recommendation of the Royal Commission that the Council should have lay members and a lay chairman. If its first report is suggestive of its future, this group is likely to manifest its fearless and high-principled character by speaking sternly to newspapers on trivial subjects.

The Nieman Reports, the Press Institute statements, A. J. Liebling's "Wayward Press," Robert Lasch in the *Progressive,* occasional studies by schools of journalism, these are all we have in this country. They are too casual and limited, and, since most of them are directed at the press, they do not perform one function that the Commission on the Freedom of the Press regarded as essential: they do not "educate the people as to the aspirations which they ought to have for the press."

Your own efforts to act as a critical agency have come to nothing. You appointed a committee in 1949 "to examine the desirability of sponsoring an appraisal of the self-improvement possibilities of American newspapers." The Committee reported in 1950 as follows: "Our Committee recognizes and reiterates that the American Society of Newspaper Editors is, itself, and must be, a continuing committee of the whole on self-examination and self-improvement. But, in addition, we urge the Society to call upon its Board of Directors to take whatever action may be necessary from time to time to clarify understanding of American newspapers by the public, and to keep editors alert to their responsibilities in fulfilling the public's right to an adequate, independent newspaper press."

That sounds as though it was written by a public relations man. In these sonorous sentences we hear the cadence of the Psalms.

The great issues of our time are peace and freedom. A new critical agency might appraise the performance of the newspapers in correcting, or contributing to, our vast confusion on these subjects. We know that the peoples of the earth are now equipped to turn one another into radioactive cinders. Can you say that the press has given Americans the material they need to reach a conclusion on the course they should follow, on the choice between co-existence and no existence, the choice between seeking peace through purchase and intimidation and seeking it through total, enforceable disarmament, the choice between competing nationalisms and world law?

And what of freedom in the garrison state? Since most of you take the official line, that the only important fact of life is our imminent danger from international conspiracy, most of you have watched the erosion of freedom without a twinge. When the official line permitted, you have sallied forth, as when you gallantly led the troops from the rear in a belated attack on Senator McCarthy. You have filled the air with warnings of the sinister figures on the Left, but have printed almost nothing about the fat cats on the Right. You have allowed things to get to such a pass that some government departments now have guidance clinics in which the employee is taught how not to look like a security risk. Look at the Passport Division, interfering with the travel of Americans on their lawful occasions; at the Attorney-General's list, ruining the lives of thousands on the basis of hearsay; at the Post Office Department, saving us from *Pravda* and Aristophanes; at the State Department, adding the name of Corsi to those of Davies and Service and countless others. See the blacklist spreading in industry, merging with proposals that American Communists should be starved to death. Listen to the wire-tapping, to the cry of Fifth Amendment Communist, to the kept witnesses roaming the land. The most distressing part of it is not that these things happen, but that the free press of this country appears to regard them as matters of routine.

You are educators, whether you like it or not. You make the views that people have of public affairs. No competition can shake you from that position. You will lose it only if you neglect or abandon it. As the number of papers per community declines, the responsibility of each one that remains increases. This is a responsibility that is discharged by being a newspaper, by giving the news. The editorial function is to make sure that it is given in such a way that it can be understood. The people must see the alternatives before them; otherwise they cannot be enlightened.

Enlightenment means telling the people where they are in

time and space. It means engaging in systematic criticism. The criticism of current affairs has to be made in the light of some standard. This must be something more than a set of partisan slogans. The standard by which the American press must judge current events is derived from an understanding of and sympathy with the deepest aspirations of the American people, those for peace and freedom. A press that serves its country in this way need have no concern about the future.

April 21, 1955

PART II: *EDUCATION*

Introduction: EDUCATION

The civilization we seek is the Civilization of the Dialogue. The educational system should prepare us for it. The university should be a paradigm of it. The university should be a center of independent thought and criticism. The President of a university should fix his mind on this goal and reject all other ambitions for his institution.

This is a brief summary of Part II of this book. *A Message to the Young Generation* is from my farewell address to the students of the University of Chicago. In attempting to state what the duty of the university graduate is it does not go as far as Woodrow Wilson, but it tends in that direction. When he was President of Princeton he said, "The object of a university is to make young gentlemen as unlike their fathers as possible."

The Kenyon lecture on morals, religion, and higher education seems to me to offer an inadequate solution of the problem that it sets out to solve. But I have been able to think of nothing better. In practice a university that wants to obtain the services of the best men in their fields will find it quite as impossible to ask a qualified specialist whether he takes morals and religion seriously as to ask him what his moral standards and religious convictions are. The lecture must therefore be regarded as an exhortation—let us take these things seriously—rather than a prescription of the methods by which a university could actually see to it that serious attention was given to morals and religion.

The lectures at the University of Uppsala seem to me more satisfactory. The dilemma with which they deal has been largely ignored; yet it really is the central issue in education today. We have been so preoccupied with getting everybody into school and providing the staff and equipment necessary for this purpose that we have had no time to think about what we are going to do with all these young people when we get them into the educational system. The deterioration of the system under the impact of the numbers already in it has seemed to us so drastic and so irreversible that we have decided to rationalize what we could not remedy. The rationalizations we have developed are dangerous; for, if we are satisfied with them, they will prevent us from moving on, when we can, from schooling to education. The fact is that we must educate everybody, and that this requirement is not met by getting everybody into school.

We are now excited about two aspects of the educational situation: how we shall get the money to pay for the buildings and teachers we need; and how we shall get the scientists, engineers, and technicians we want. The first question is absurd; for we spend more money on liquor, tobacco, and cosmetics than we do on education. The second question is trivial; for we know perfectly well that the way we get people interested in anything in our society is to offer interesting financial rewards. A few years ago fifty percent of the graduate of engineering schools were not going into engineering. If the proportion entering the profession is higher now, it is because the financial prospects of engineers are brighter now.

The basic educational question is, how are we to equip every citizen to cope to the best of his ability with the problems of the modern world? To answer this question we shall have to think a great deal more about what is to go in our educational institutions than we have been willing to up to now. We need a thoroughgoing revision of the institutions we have, and, as the last pages of "The Democratic Dilemma" suggest, we need at the summit an altogether new kind of institution.

The speech on *Education and Independent Thought* is an attempt to straighten out the relations of the university to the community. The thesis is that the community needs independent thought and criticism and that the university has been established to provide these things. Everything follows from this, including the definition of the role of trustees and regents. The speech was written at a time when various public bodies and private organizations were trying to control the universities in various misguided ways. I believe—perhaps I am misguided—that the thesis of this speech offers the only hope of resisting attempts to complete the transformation of our universities into service stations.

I do not believe that the plight of the university administrator portrayed in the first of the two speeches about him is overdrawn. The only kind of man who can cheerfully administer a large university today is one who is not interested in education. A man who is interested will find himself constantly frustrated. I am convinced, as the second speech shows, that federalization alone can provide a remedy. Only in a small unit can the man who wants to "get things done" follow the prescription of patience and procure the consensus that satisfactory administration requires.

The Administrator Reconsidered suggests that the administration of foundations is in some respects more difficult than that of universities. Although the idea of a university is not very clear, most people have some idea of one. Most people have no idea what a foundation is. Congressional investigations have obscured what little comprehension there was. They have also tended to intimidate the officers and trustees of foundations. The temptation to the administrator of a foundation to become a bureaucratic officeholder is almost irresistible. Yet it would seem that the only justification for the foundations is that they, as experts in philanthropy, might be able to do things that need to be done but that nobody else will venture to try.

The distribution of charitable funds on a kind of *per capita* basis to established institutions for conventional purposes is little more than a clerical job. It will support neither the overhead costs of the foundations nor their claim before the Cox Committee that they are the indispensable risk capital of philanthropy. The vision of the end, to the administrator of a foundation, would mean that he would be bold and imaginative in proposing the expenditure of funds in terms of needs not generally felt—but nonetheless real—or not likely to be met, or met in the near future, in the ordinary course of charitable giving.

The speeches in the next section indicate some of the difficulties that foundations that try to be bold and imaginative are likely to encounter.

ONE

A MESSAGE TO THE YOUNG GENERATION

The greatest difference between your time in college and my own is the popularization in the intervening years of the works of Freud. Far be it from me to decry the significance of this writer. But I must say that he has had, as it seems to me, an unfortunate effect upon your conversation and upon the standards by which you judge yourselves and others. A graduate student in psychology told me last year that in her opinion 99 per cent of the people of this country were abnormal. In addition to providing an interesting definition of normality, this suggested to me that the ordinary difficulties of growing up and becoming human, from which the race has suffered for a million years, had taken on a kind of clinical character that I could not help hoping was exaggerated. Whenever I have visited with student groups, I have been impressed by your determined insistence that you were neurotic and your resentment at my suggestion that you looked perfectly all right to me.

On the principle laid down by Gilbert and Sullivan that when everybody is somebody, nobody is anybody: if everybody is abnormal, we don't need to worry about anybody. Nor should I be prepared to admit that a serious interest in being educated, the characteristic that distinguishes the students of the University of Chicago from all others, is necessarily neurotic. It may be in these times in this country somewhat eccentric, but it seems to me an amiable eccentricity, and one that should be encouraged. The whole doctrine that we must adjust ourselves to our environment, which I take to be the prevailing doctrine of American education, seems to me radically erroneous. Our mission here on earth is to change our environment, not to adjust ourselves to it. If we become maladjusted in the process, so much the worse for the environment. If we have to choose between Sancho Panza and Don Quixote, let us by all means choose Don Quixote. The flat conformity of American life and thought, toward which all pressures in this country converge, raises the only doubt one may have about democracy, which is whether it is possible to combine the rule of the majority with that independence of character, conduct, and thought which the progress of any society requires.

One of the most interesting questions about the higher learning in America is this: why is it that the boy who on June 15 receives his degree, eager, enthusiastic, outspoken, idealistic, reflective, and independent, is on the following September 15, or even on June 16, except at Chicago, dull, uninspired, shifty, cautious, pliable, and attired in a single-breasted grey flannel suit? Why are the graduates of the great American universities indistinguishable, even by their grammar, from the mass of the population who have never had their advantages? Their grammar may perhaps be accounted for by the deficiencies of the American schools, the ineradicable marks of which are borne by our fellow countrymen to their dying day. But what about the intellectual interest, the willingness and ability to reason, the independence of thought and character, the

> Spirit of youth, alive, unchanging,
> Under whose feet the years are cast,
> Heir to an ageless empire ranging
> Over the future and the past—

What about that? Why are the alumni organizations of the country, except that of Chicago, dedicated to the affectionate perpetuation of all the wrong things about their universities? Why do the massed graduates of American universities behave in the same way on the same kind of occasions as the massed followers of the most celebrated cultural institution of my native city, the Dodgers?

The answer must lie in the relative weakness of higher education compared with the forces that make everybody think and act like everybody else. Those forces beat upon the individual from his birth up on almost a twenty-four-hour-a-day basis and constitute the greatest obstacle with which the schools have to contend; so that it can now be seriously argued that since education cannot cope with the comic book it should absorb it and substitute elevating and instructive comic books for textbooks. The horrid prospect that television opens before us, with nobody speaking and nobody reading, suggests that a bleak and torpid epoch may lie ahead, which, if it lasts long enough, will gradually, according to the principles of evolution, produce a population indistinguishable from the lower forms of plant life. Astronomers of the University of Chicago have detected something that looks like moss growing on Mars. I am convinced that Mars was once inhabited by rational beings like ourselves, who had the misfortune, some thousands of years ago, to invent television.

The forces that beat upon the American citizen from infancy become really serious when he finishes his formal schooling and has to think about earning a living and getting along in the world. How will those who have jobs to offer and prestige to confer feel about him if he does not merge imperceptibly with the scenery? How far will he get if he does not adjust himself to his environment? I hasten to say that I am for tact, politeness, and good manners. I would not for the world be taken as urging you to be offensive or holier-than-thou or carry a chip on your shoulder or fail to distinguish between matters of etiquette and matters of principle. You may even wear a single-breasted grey flannel suit if you find it becoming. But to adjust yourselves to brutality, inhumanity, injustice, and stupidity, of which the world is full, though it is easy, and may look profitable, is, I must warn you, habit-forming, and will make out of you at the last characters that you would shudder to think of now.

My observation leads me to think that happiness lies in the fullest use of one's highest powers. Of course it is folly to talk of the fullest use of a man's highest powers if he is starving to death. You are in little danger of starving to death, at least you are if a world catastrophe can be avoided. Your advantages are such that you have a decided superiority over the great majority of your fellow citizens when it comes to the sheer business of staying alive. Your problem lies in the moral and intellectual realm, in achieving the feeling that you have made the most of yourselves, that you have done the best you could, and that you have not let down yourselves or your fellow men.

Here I hope that you will follow the example of your University. I still think, as I have thought for many years, that the motto of the University should be that line from Walt Whitman, "Solitary, singing in the West, I strike up for a new world."

Our lives are overshadowed now by the threat of impending doom. If you were neurotic, I could not blame you. To what extent the threat of impending doom grows out of our ignorance and immorality, and to what extent it grows out of the ignorance and immorality of the Russians I do not pretend to know. I confess, too, that I have a lifelong hatred of war that perhaps makes it impossible for me to have a rational view of the present situation. War has always seemed to me the ultimate wickedness, the ultimate stupidity. And if this was true in less enlightened times, when the best we could do was to slaughter one another with TNT, it is plain as day now, when, thanks to the progress of the higher learning, we can wipe out thousands of innocent people at one blow, and be wiped out ourselves in the same way. I am not a pacifist. I grant that when a great power is loose in the world seeking whom it may destroy, it is necessary to prepare to defend our country against it.

Yet the goal toward which all history tends is peace, not peace through the medium of war, not peace through a process of universal intimidation, not peace through a program of mutual impoverishment, not peace by any means that leaves the world too frightened or too weak to go on fighting, but peace pure and simple, based on that will to peace which has animated the overwhelming majority of mankind through countless ages. This will to peace does not arise out of a cowardly desire to preserve one's life and property, but out of a conviction that the fullest development of the highest powers of men can be achieved only in a world at peace.

War, particularly modern war, is a horrible disaster. If this is the destiny prepared for us, we must meet it as best we can. But at least we should have no illusions about it. There is a certain terrifying lightheartedness underlying the talk about war today. Each political party is belaboring the other not because it is too warlike, but because it is too peaceful. Men in public life are being crucified because they are suspected of trying to keep the peace. The presidents of the greatest universities have met and enthusiastically voted to abandon the higher learning so that the universities may become part of the military establishment. By endless reiteration of the slogan, "America must be strong," we have been able to put a stop to our mental processes altogether and to forget what strength is.

We appear to believe that strength consists of masses of men and machines. I do not deny that they have their role. But surely the essential ingredients of strength are trained intelligence, love of country, the understanding of its ideals, and above all, a conviction of the justice of our cause. Since men of good will can regard war as conceivable only as a last resort, they must be convinced that all channels of negotiation have been kept open till the last moment and that their own government has sought in good faith, and without consideration of face or prestige, to prevent the outbreak of war. Men of good will must be convinced that they are not fighting to maintain colonialism, feudalism, or any other form of entrenched injustice. And since it is obvious to the merest simpleton that war must come sooner or later to a world of anarchy, men of good will would hope that their own government would proclaim its desire to transform the United Nations from a loose association of independent states into an organization that could adopt and enforce world law.

There seems to be something about contemporary civilization that produces a sense of aimlessness. Why do university presidents cheerfully welcome the chance to devote their institutions to military preparations? They are of course patriotic; but in addition I think they feel that education is a boring, confusing, difficult matter that nobody cares very much about anyway, whereas getting ready for war is simple, clear, definite, and respectable. Can it be that modern men can have a sense of purpose only if they believe that other men are getting ready to kill them? If this is true, western civilization is surely neurotic, and fatally so.

You are getting an education infinitely better than that which my generation, the generation that now rules the world, had open to it. You have had the chance to discern the purpose of human life and human society. Your predecessors in this place, now scattered all over the world, give us some warrant for hoping that as you go out to join them you will bear with you the same spark that they have carried, which, if carefully tended, may yet become the light that shall illumine the world.

February 21, 1951

TWO

MORALS, RELIGION, AND HIGHER EDUCATION

This essay is an inquiry into problems that are among the hardest in education. I cannot pretend that I have solved any of them. The inquiry will take us through some of the solutions that have been offered. If in the process it appears that these solutions are inadequate, I beg the reader not to despair; for it may be possible to discover solutions that may be workable and sound. I believe that higher education can make a unique contribution to morals and religion. I do not believe that it can make some of the contributions expected of it, and I think that these expectations obscure the real purposes and achievements of higher education. The object of this essay must therefore be rather more to clear the ground than to erect a building. I can regard the building attempted here as at best a very modest structure, which will accomplish more than I am entitled to hope for it if it serves as temporary shelter to those who may design the ultimate edifice.

The essay uses the words "morals," "religion," and "higher education" in a definite sense. The sense may be wrong, but it is consistently employed. By morals I mean good habits. Good habits are those which are good for the organism in question. To know what is good for an organism, you have to know the nature of that organism. If man is an animal like any other, then there is no reason why we should expect him to have habits any different from the other animals. For by good habits we do not mean obedience to conventions. That lies in the sphere of etiquette, rather than morals, and we are concerned here with morals.

For example, the Kinsey Report has no moral significance. The Report seems to proceed on the assumption that, since man is an animal like any other, and since morals are purely conventional, a moral revolution may be effected by showing that we do not live according to the conventions we profess. To show that men do not live according to the conventions they profess merely shows that they do not live according to the conventions they profess. It shows nothing at all about what is good for man or what is bad for him. The fact that a great many men may be doing what is bad for them is neither new nor relevant. A man may change a convention by getting the leaders of society to join him in breaking it. A man cannot change bad to good even if he gets all his fellow-men to conspire with him.

By religion I mean belief in and obedience to God. This may not require adherence to a church or creed; but it demands religious faith. Faith is not reason, but it is something more than a vague, sentimental desire to do good and be good. The problem of faith and reason has agitated mankind for centuries, and I could not deal with it here, even if I knew how. But the kind of religion I am talking about is one that is sustained by both reason and faith. We see in St. Augustine's *Confessions* the way in which a man may come to the sort of religious conviction that has meaning. St. Augustine's conversion followed after tremendous wrestling with the intellectual difficulties of Christianity and was prepared by the conquest of those difficulties.

By higher education I mean that education which takes place in institutions beyond the secondary level as secondary education is usually defined. I mean the education that is given by the colleges and universities of this country. I do not believe that these institutions are properly organized. The college should occupy the area now uneasily filled by the last two years of high school and the first two years of college, and the university should begin its work at the beginning of the conventional junior year in college. But for the purposes of this essay I am willing to regard all the colleges of the United States as offering higher education. I am willing to include all universities, too, even though I believe that a university is a place where all professors and all students are engaged in independent study, and in this view a true university has not yet arisen in our country.

We are concerned, then, with what goes on or with what should go on in certain institutions, in institutions of a certain kind. And it is important to notice that what goes on or should go on in these institutions is severely limited to what can go on in them. What can go on in them is in part determined by the age of the students with whom they have to deal and by the length of time that they spend in the institutions. At any university, if an alumnus "succeeds" in later life, it is customary for the university to take the credit for it; if he goes to the penitentiary, it is said that he was bad material and should never have been admitted. President Truman's Commission on Higher Education sees the student going to college in the moral and intellectual state of the newborn babe and graduating four, or even two, years later as a mature and autonomous member of society. The Commission, like most people who know far less about education, places on the educational institution a responsibility for the total development of the individual by starting and ending with the wrong assumptions.

The assumption that a college freshman has no habits is in obvious contradiction to the facts of life. The assumption that if he has no habits, or, if his habits are all bad, he can acquire in four years a set of good habits that will last all his life is certainly naïve. My guess is that eighteen is a greater age than we who are past it are willing to admit. It is flattering to us, and it makes our work easier, to feel that our students are children who can do nothing and learn little without our help and supervision; but to suppose that a boy or girl of eighteen has been unaffected by his home and by society is not merely factually inaccurate; it gives higher education a false conception of its task and its possibilities; and it must contribute to that prolongation of adolescence which is so distressing a feature of American life.

We are concerned here, then, with what certain institutions can do in a certain period of time with certain people of a certain age.[1] And in each institution there will be a certain number of these young people, and usually a number larger than one per instructor. Rousseau's *Émile* contains some interesting educational suggestions, but it can help us in the solution of few of the practical problems that affect an educational system: Émile had a tutor and never went to school.[2] We are discussing what can be done in scholastic institutions at a certain level.

John Stuart Mill faced this question in his inaugural address at St. Andrew's. He said: "No one can dispense with an education directed expressly to the moral as well as the intellectual part of his being. Such education, so far as it is direct, is either moral or religious; and these may either be treated as distinct, or as different aspects of the same thing. The subject we are now considering is not education as a whole, but scholastic education, and we must keep in view the inevitable limitations of what schools and universities can do. It is beyond their power to educate morally or religiously. Moral and religious education consist in training the feelings and the daily habits; and these are, in the main, beyond the sphere and inaccessible to the control of public education. It is the home, the family, which gives us the moral or religious education we really receive; and this is completed, and modified, sometimes for the better, often for the worse, by society, and the opinions and feelings with which we are there surrounded."

So Cardinal Newman insisted over and over again that the purpose of a university was intellectual and not moral. The utilitarian philosopher and the Catholic theologian came to the same conclusion, though perhaps for different reasons. To the role of the family Newman adds that of the church, which, characteristically, Mill does not mention in his discussion of moral and religious education. They both hold that it is beyond the power of higher education to educate morally and religiously. Both Newman and Mill view the world about them as containing various agencies and institutions, each with a purpose of its own. The sphere of the family or the church is not the sphere of educational institutions; the sphere of educational institutions is not that of the family or the church.

Mill and Newman were writing in the nineteenth century, when both church and family were more effective in their spheres than they are today. Would their conclusion be any different now, when, we are told, the family is disintegrating and the church is dying? I think not. Even if they assumed that the family was going to pieces and the church on the way to extinction, Newman and Mill would hardly suppose that the way to revive these institutions was to turn over their functions to another agency. This could only guarantee the destruction of the family and the church. And, if the attempt were made to turn their functions over to the educational system, it would guarantee the increasing confusion of that agency. If we can find out what the proper function of the educational system is, we shall discover at the same time, I am sure, that the performance of that function will require all the attention and intelligence that the educational system can command.

Mill emphasizes another point: some phases of human development are determined by the impact of society in adult life. In our time the impact of society, particularly as it makes itself felt through what are called the media of mass communication, of which Mill and Newman were fortunately ignorant, is, I think, the most important factor in moral and cultural development. I do not see how any educational system can be expected to cope with the comic book, the radio, the motion picture, the slick-paper magazine, television, and the sensational press. The tremendous skill and the enormous resources available to these moral and cultural agencies make them more influential in molding the lives of our people than the whole educational system. And even if the educational system had more money and more skill, as it certainly should have, there appears to be a kind of Gresham's law of culture, under which bad stuff drives out good. Probably because of original sin, human beings seem to prefer demoralization to improvement.

The usual answer to this is that we shall educate human beings to be better and to prefer to be better than worse. This seems to me to overlook the limited time that the educational system has at its disposal and the limited influence that it can therefore have upon the lives of those who, even while they are temporarily committed to its care, are soaking up through every pore poisons transmitted by every device that the triumphs of science and technology now make it possible to subject them to.

An officer of the General Electric Company has lately commented on the cultural benefits conferred upon us by television. He said that the principal market for television sets was saloons and that therefore the contribution of this triumph of science and technology to the advance of civilization was more booze, less fresh air, and the same old ball game.

In *A Study of History* Mr. Toynbee deals at length with the stumbling blocks that have prevented universal free education from ushering in a new era of happiness and well-being for Western society. The dangerous consequence of the introduction of universal free education in Great Britain in 1870, Toynbee argues, was the triumph of yellow journalism—and later the movies—which succeeded in creating an intellectual tyranny more deadening than the illiteracy from which free schooling had rescued the masses.[3] The only remedy to this situation, Toynbee continues, is to raise the level of mass cultivation.[4]

We must heartily agree with Mr. Toynbee that it is desirable to raise the level of mass cultivation. From the point of view of Mr. Toynbee's aims, universal liberal education, rather than universal schooling, is indicated. But to hope that even the best training in criticism can cope with the constant storm of triviality and propaganda that now beats upon the citizen seems to me to expect too much of any educational system. Such training should certainly be given, and given to everybody. But an educational system cannot reform a society, and Mr. Toynbee is calling for nothing less.

I can pursue this subject no further, for that way madness lies. I can only assume that the educational system will continue to do its best in the hope that some day a sort of mass conversion will overtake our people, and they will want to be better. If they do not want to be better, the educational system cannot make them so. And the educational system cannot make them want to be so. All it can do is to offer an opportunity and, perhaps, an example of which those who wish to swim against the tide can avail themselves. It is, of course, imperative that this opportunity and this example should constantly be held before our people.

Let us return to Newman and Mill. They do not say that moral and religious education is unimportant. On the contrary, they both feel that moral and religious education is more important than intellectual education. So do I. The question is not whether moral and religious education is important, but what colleges and universities can do about it. No one would favor a nation of highly intelligent and well-trained robbers, murderers, thieves, arsonists, and forgers. And no one would contend that knowledge of the arts and sciences automatically leads to the development of good moral habits.

Aristotle said that it is impossible to be wise without being good, and impossible to be good without being wise. But this cannot be taken to mean that it is impossible to be good without qualifying for the Ph.D. degree. We all know good scholars who are bad men; and I have known some illiterates who seemed good to me. Aristotle meant that it is impossible to be good without being prudent, or practically wise, because the imprudent man does not know how to adjust means to ends; and it is impossible to be prudent, or practically wise, without being good, because the bad man is seeking the wrong ends. Though prudence is a habit of the mind, it seems to me that habit of the mind which higher education is least qualified and least likely to teach. The development of prudence requires long experience and reflection. Aristotle said that young men should not listen to lectures on moral philosophy, because they have had no experience; they would have only the vaguest and most abstract notions of what was under discussion. As I indicated earlier, college and university students are likely to be more mature than we think they are. They are not blank tablets upon which the teacher can write anything he pleases. They have habits, and many, if not most, of them have learned something of religion. But by saying that they are more mature than we think they are I do not mean to say they are mature. They are not experienced adults. It is hard to disagree with Aristotle's principle that subjects that require experience do not convey their full meaning to the inexperienced.

For this reason we may lament the low estate of the education of adults in this country. Moral and political philosophy, history, and literature yield up their full lessons only to those who have had the experience to comprehend them. If they are taught to the inexperienced and never taught again, they are never comprehended. A boy will read a few plays of Shakespeare in high school and never look at them for the rest of his life. Shakespeare remains for him a quaint ancient writer who did not know how to spell very well, but who has managed to leave us a large number of quotations for funeral orations and Fourth of July addresses. This does not mean that Shakespeare should not be taught in high school. It means that if he is read only in high school, we never get more than a fraction of what he has to give us. My favorite illustration is *Macbeth*. When I taught *Macbeth* to students in a preparatory school, it was a blood-and-thunder story. It was a good blood-and-thunder story, and one well worth teaching; but it was a blood-and-thunder story still. *Macbeth* can mean to us what it meant to Shakespeare only if we have had enough experience, vicarious or otherwise, of marriage and ambition to understand the issues and their implications.

These considerations suggest that the curriculum in our schools and colleges is upside down. It is assumed that children are primarily interested in the life about them and that subjects dealing with the life about them command their attention and enlist their understanding; hence the increasing prominence of the social studies in the schools. Nothing in my experience suggests that children are more interested in American history than in arithmetic and the stories of ancient Greece. Those subjects which are commonly supposed to be too abstract for the young, like mathematics, grammar, logic, astronomy, and music, are the best subjects for the young precisely because they are abstract. Their comprehension requires no experience or maturity. I see no escape from the proposition that subjects that require experience and maturity cannot be profitably taught to the inexperienced and immature.

At any rate it seems to me that higher education probably cannot teach prudence or practical wisdom, that habit of the mind by which we select the right means to the end. Nor can it, I believe, teach good habits of action. It cannot teach morals.

The moral virtues are habits, and habits are formed by acts. We can have no assurance that courses in elementary, intermediate, and advanced goodness will be followed by good acts. In fact, such courses seem likely to induce precisely the opposite behavior. The boarding school in the country, and to some extent the college in a small town, may be able to prevent its students from the habitual performance of acts so bad that they violate the law or outrage the conventions. But even this opportunity is denied the metropolitan university, half the students of which live at home, far from the benevolent influence of the dean of men and the dean of women. In any event this kind of control must be of the most superficial and negative order. It will not do to say that higher education should try to prevent crime. What we are seeking to discover is the means by which higher education can promote the formation of good habits; it can hardly hope to do so by courses in how to be good.

Nor can it hope to do so by means of extra-curricular activities, at least on that industrial or "big-time" scale with which we in America are familiar. Under this system a few highly trained but somewhat under-paid experts go through the discipline and sometimes suffer the fate of the gladiators of old while the rest of the college observes their conduct on Saturday afternoons in the spirit of a Roman holiday. I confess I am unable to see what this has to do with morals, religion, or higher education, except as to the experts referred to. They indeed may develop some habits, and some of the habits may be good. The four cardinal virtues are traditionally supposed to be courage, temperance, justice, and prudence; and the athlete may be compelled, in so far as he is an athlete, to give some appearance of them all.

The courage that is required to meet the shock of a 225-pound steelworker imported from Gary, and the temperance required at the training table, and the justice required to obey the rules, and the prudence required to select the right means to the end of victory doubtless bear some relation to the courage, temperance, justice, and prudence that moralists had in mind when they isolated and described the cardinal virtues. But the effect of the activities of the experts on the moral character of the rest of the college must be slight at best. My class never saw Yale win a big game, and it was said of the coach of that time that he had conferred one inestimable moral benefit upon the student body: he had taught them not to bet—or at least not to bet on Yale. I do not depreciate this contribution; for temperance and prudence would seem to forbid gambling. But this contribution, important as it is, seems to me negligible in contrast to the enormous expenditure of time, money, effort, and interest that went into the acquisition of it.

Even if extra-curricular activities had the decisively beneficial influence on character that their devotees claim for them, that would hardly help us to answer the question of the special role of higher education in the formation of character; for extra-curricular activities could be conducted more effectively if there were no curriculum at all. They could be and are conducted in YMCA's or Boy Scout encampments, at country clubs and among the Campfire Girls. Extra-curricular activities are not the peculiar property of educational institutions, nor do they serve to clarify the peculiar part that educational institutions can play in the formation of character.

Higher education cannot hope to make students good by compulsory religious exercises. If a college or university has decided to be secular, in the sense that it requires no religious tests of its students or faculty, if it wants to appeal to those of no faith, of little faith, and many faiths, it cannot compel worship. It may compel attendance; my classmates came to morning chapel with overcoats over their pajamas and coughed the speaker down.[5] After five years of coughing, compulsory chapel was abolished. There was moaning among some of the trustees, alumni, and faculty; but a college cannot have it both ways. It cannot hold itself out as secular and then demand that its members go through religious ceremonies as a condition of being allowed to continue as members.

The great majority of the endowed colleges and universities of this country have long since passed from under the control of the religious groups that founded them; and public institutions seem required by the Constitution to be secular. Yet it must be admitted that religion is of the greatest moral importance. If the whole world practiced Aristotle's *Ethics*, the whole world would be much better off than it is today. But I doubt if any single man, to say nothing of the whole world, can practice Aristotle's *Ethics* without the support and inspiration of religious faith. This Aristotle himself seemed to recognize; for the ideal man whom he holds up to our admiration is one who is almost divine. The modern critic is inclined to scoff at the Aristotelian dictum that men are rational animals. It is no longer fashionable to refer to the rationality of man. But Aristotle was saying not merely that men are rational but also that they are animal.[6] Because men are animal, because the flesh is weak and life is hard, the moral virtues cannot be consistently practiced without divine aid.

Metaphysics and what is called natural theology deal with the ultimate questions. But intellectual history reveals nothing so clearly as their inadequacy for the task. The existence and nature of God, the character and destiny of the human soul, and the salvation of man are problems that remain obscure in the light of natural reason. Or consider human life without religion and history without providence. A perfect theory of democracy can be made out of the metaphysical and ethical writings of Aristotle. But as he himself did not have the fortitude to follow his premises to their conclusions and admit all men to participation in their own government, so it is improbable that the practice of democracy now or in the future can be achieved merely by the demonstration of its reasonableness. Men, simply because they are men, are unlikely to find within themselves the power that can bring the good life and the good state to pass. As Reinhold Niebuhr pointed out in his Gifford lectures, all anthropocentric ethical doctrines fail at this point: they overlook the fallen nature of man and assume that without grace he can reach a terrestrial end to which, almost by definition, no being with such a nature can ever attain.

No one could have been more conscious of the dependence of morals upon religion than Cardinal Newman, and it was he who said that the purpose of a university was intellectual, not moral. Our question is not whether religion is indispensable to the good life, but whether the educational system can give us everything that is indispensable to the good life. If a college cannot make its students religious, it cannot, to that extent, make them good.

Why cannot higher education make its students religious? Why can it not exact a religious commitment from all entering students and apply religious tests determining or affecting their progress through and graduation from the institution? Why can it not insist that all members of the faculty shall be members in good standing of Christian churches and shall perform their religious duties with the same regularity and obligation as they now perform their teaching duties?

Perhaps a college could do these things, but it would be unfortunate if it did. Faith is one of the theological virtues; it may be deserved, but it is not earned. It is a gift of God. Those who have been denied this gift should not be denied educational opportunities.

As to the professors, let us imagine that the college or university has a choice between a man who is a third-rate historian or physicist but an ardent believer and one who is a first-rate historian or physicist and an atheist. Which should it choose? I approach this question with some diffidence, for I am not at all sure of the answer. John Stuart Mill had an answer. He said: "The moral or religious influence which an university can exercise, consists less in any express teaching, than in the pervading tone of the place. Whatever it teaches, it should teach as penetrated by a sense of duty; it should present all knowledge as chiefly a means to worthiness of life, given for the double purpose of making each of us practically useful to his fellow-creatures, and of elevating the character of the species itself; exalting and dignifying our nature."

Mill says that the moral and religious influence of a university consists in its pervading tone. If the pervading tone is moral and religious, moral and religious influence will follow. But how is the pervading tone set? The pervading tone of higher education must be set by those who guide its destinies and teach its students. If they are moral and religious, the tone may be that which Mill would like to hear. If they are not, the tone may be something else altogether.

Since we are agreed that it is more important to be good than to be intellectual, and that it is hard, if not impossible, to be good without being religious, and since we want higher education to exert a moral and religious influence through its pervading tone, it would seem to follow that men should not be appointed to the faculties of colleges and universities unless they are moral and religious men. Yet we know that every day men are appointed to faculties after a most painstaking investigation of their intellectual attainments, but without any inquiry into their moral habits or their religious beliefs. I do it every day myself. We do not ask whether the prospective appointee is afflicted with scientism, skepticism, or secularism. We do not request him to state whether he believes in God or whether or not he thinks morals are indistinguishable from the mores and are relative, like the mores, to time and place. We ask what his training has been, what his record was, what his publications are, and what are the prospects of his publishing any more. We ask, in short, whether he has discovered any truths in his specialty, and whether he can be expected to seek for and, perhaps, discover additional truths. It would be regarded as an impertinence in a secular institution to ask a prospective faculty member about anything outside his specialty, unless, of course, rumors of flagrant immorality likely to embarrass the college had reached the president's ears. These would have to be inquired into and all fears on this score set at rest. But everybody would be shocked at the suggestion that it is proper to investigate a man's beliefs, or to ask what, if anything, he stands for.

It is perfectly fair for higher education to say that its aim is the pursuit and transmission of truth. For this purpose the institution is divided into departments, subdepartments, and subsections of subdepartments. The assumption is that nobody can discover the whole truth but that by a collective effort on the part of specialists in many fields the institution as such may get closer to the whole truth than any single individual.

The reason it is perfectly fair for a college or university to say that its aim is the pursuit and transmission of truth is that in our society only these institutions have this aim. So Mill said of morals and religion: "What is special to an university on these subjects belongs chiefly, like the rest of its work, to the intellectual department. An university exists for the purpose of laying open to each succeeding generation, as far as the conditions of the case admit, the accumulated treasure of the thoughts of mankind."

In this view a college or university is a place where people think. And the test of all its work, the test of the work of professors and students, the test of every course and every research project is: how much thought does it require? But can this be all? Does this mean that as long as there is thought it makes no difference what is thought about, or are some things more important to think about than others?

The practices of higher education in America do not conform to the views of Mill, to say nothing of meeting the further question I have raised concerning the relative importance of things to be thought about. The three types of curriculum current in this country may be called the life-activities centered curriculum, the student-interest centered curriculum, and the professor-interest centered curriculum. The life-activities centered curriculum is exemplified by the course of study of a women's college, which is based on a job analysis of the diaries of several hundred mature women. The categories of the activities of these women constitute the structure of the college curriculum, although women, perhaps, ought to do and may even be doing things that these mature women did not do. The student-interest centered curriculum, apparently on the theory that it is hopeless to try to understand education or to figure out what an education should be, simply takes the expression of interest on the part of the student as revealing what he should study, for who knows what he should study, anyway? The professor-interest centered curriculum is the more usual variety. Each professor and each department want the whole time of the student so that he can be thoroughly trained in the professor's or the department's specialty. Since it is obviously impossible for the student's whole time to be spent in this way, the curriculum is determined by a process of pulling, hauling, and logrolling; and finally emerges as a sort of checkerboard across which the bewildered student moves, absorbing from each square, it is hoped, a little of something that each professor or each department has to offer him.

None of these courses of study has any necessary connection with thinking. The activities of mature women may have had little to do with thinking. Some students may not be interested in thought. And I have heard of professors and departments who believed that their function was to cram their students with information. It is hard to contemplate such courses of study without agreeing with Henry Adams, who said, "The chief wonder of education is that it does not ruin everybody concerned in it, teachers and taught."

If we insist that colleges and universities should be devoted to thinking, and if we insist that they should, if possible, think about important things, we may perhaps find the way in which higher education may make its unique contribution to morals and religion. Most of our educational institutions are and will probably remain secular, in the sense that they are not controlled by any church and are open to everybody regardless of his religious faith or lack of it. But there is another kind of secularism that besets the higher learning in America, and that is secularism in the sense in which we say that religion is insignificant, it is outmoded, it is equivalent to superstition. This kind of secularism higher education can and should repel. If a college or university is going to think and to think about important things, then it must think about religion. It is perhaps not necessary that all the faculty should be religious; it would be desirable that most of them, at least, should take religion seriously.

The same is true of morals. If a college or university is to think and think about important things, then it must think about morals, for we have admitted throughout that morals are most important. It may not be necessary that all the faculty should be good; it would be desirable that most of them, at least, take goodness seriously.

If we grant that the purpose of higher education is to think and to think about important things for the purpose of learning as much of the truth as possible about these things and transmitting it to each succeeding generation, we see immediately that certain moral and religious consequences follow. In the first place, higher education then supplies the intellectual foundations of morals and religion. This is a contribution of the first importance, and it is, I believe, a contribution to morals and religion that only higher education can make.

As to religion, I need only refer again to St. Augustine to make the point that the resolution of intellectual difficulties seems to me, if not necessary, at least highly desirable as a prelude to or concomitant of religious faith. As to morals, habits are so much a function of the circumstances under which they were formed that we can have little assurance of their continuance in other circumstances unless the person who has the habits knows why he should retain them. As habits are formed by acts, they are broken by the cessation of these acts or by the continued performance of conflicting acts. The child carefully nurtured in good habits that he practices without comprehending the reasons for doing so is likely to fall from grace when he casts off the parental apron strings. The serious consideration of the intellectual foundations of good habits should supply him with the conviction he needs in order to keep up in adult life the good work begun in childhood.

The curriculum, then, should include the knowledge and understanding of the principles of morality. It should include both natural and sacred theology; for how can a man call himself educated who does not grasp the leading ideas that since the dawn of history have animated mankind? The institution must be committed to taking morality and religion seriously. This commitment involves a third: if the object of higher education is the truth, then, in order to take morality and religion seriously, the institution must believe that there is some truth and some discoverable truth about morality and religion. According to the dogmas of scientism, skepticism, and secularism there is no such truth. If there is truth at all, it is truth discoverable in the laboratory, by what is called the scientific method. I recently heard a minister of a Protestant church state at a public meeting that no man could tell whether a given act was right or wrong. I replied that he was a moral relativist, thinking that he would be so stung by this reproach that he might reconsider his position. Instead he proudly answered, "Of course I am a moral relativist," as though to say that anybody who is not a moral relativist is an unenlightened, unscientific, medieval reactionary.

We should all admit, I suppose, that a moral act is one performed in the right way under the right circumstances; but the notion that under some circumstances it could be right, for example, for one man to kill another with malice aforethought must mean that there is no difference between good and bad, between right and wrong, that there is no moral law and there are no moral principles that higher education can take seriously. It must mean that there are no morals; there are only the mores; and there is no religion; there is only superstition. If higher education is to take morality and religion seriously, it must repudiate these dogmas; for the truths of morality and religion never have been and never can be discovered by experiment or by any allegedly "scientific" means. Morality and religion cannot be taken seriously unless the possibility of attaining truth by philosophical inquiry and by revelation is admitted. It is necessary to believe that philosophy is something more than words and that it is possible to be rational and religious at the same time.[7]

By the commitments to which I have referred, higher education may directly contribute to the formation of character. The indirect contributions it may make are, perhaps, almost as important. These are the moral by-products of its intellectual work. The life of learning requires the support of the moral virtues; and an arduous academic career must tend to develop those virtues. Without courage or fortitude no one can long stick at the painful task of thinking and studying. Without temperance no one can resist the momentary pleasures and distractions that interfere with study. Without at least some rudimentary sort of prudence no one can allocate his time and plan his work so as to make the most of his academic opportunities. Without justice, which involves a right relation to one's teachers and fellow-students, no one can conduct himself in the academic community in a way that respects the rights of the mind. I might add that as the student owes a debt of justice to his teachers, so his teachers owe a debt of justice to him, which they do not discharge by regaling him with last year's lecture notes.

The first obligation of an intellectual institution is to set high intellectual standards and to insist on good intellectual work. There is something in Woodrow Wilson's remark that character is a by-product—a by-product of hard work well done.[8] The indirect contribution of higher education to morals cannot be made if educational institutions confer academic recognition on those who have done little more for four years than sit out their time. Habits of industry, habits of initiative, habits of tolerance, and habits of independent judgment can all be promoted by the course of study itself and by the methods by which the educational process is carried on.

If the bulk of the instruction is given by lectures, if the duty of the student is to take notes on lectures and to read textbooks, memorizing material to be regurgitated on the examinations given by the teacher who has taught the course, he may develop the habit of memory and the habit of studying the prejudices or curves of those whose favor he hopes to win. The first of these is a good and important habit, though perhaps not the best or most important of the intellectual virtues. The second is a habit valuable to salesmen, advertising men, college presidents, and others who spend their lives trying to get something from other people. But it is a habit into which most Americans seem to fall naturally; they do not need to go to college to get it. The value of the discussion method of instruction, of demanding a great deal of independent work from the student, and of a system of external examinations that requires study of the subject rather than the teacher, is that the habits of action, as well as the habits of thought and knowledge, formed by these means are closely analogous to, if they are not identical with, the four cardinal virtues.

I should add that there is a certain moral failure on the part of an educational institution that does not try to make its work something other than the accumulation of miscellaneous credits; for it seems unjust to expect the student to work hard on trivial, irrelevant, incoherent, and meaningless material. The vice of the adding-machine method of education is that it has a way of making even important subject matter seem trivial, irrelevant, incoherent, and meaningless.

There is a certain moral failure, too, on the part of an educational institution that does not allow the student to make his own the treasure of the accumulated thoughts of the race. So the failure of the elective system was a moral failure. The official historian of Harvard said of President Eliot that he had defrauded the Harvard students of their cultural heritage. The failure of vocational education is of the same variety: in the name of a specious commercial or industrial dexterity it cheats the student out of his place in the stream of human history.

An educational institution should be a community. A community must have a common aim, and the common aim of the educational community is the truth. It is not necessary that the members of the educational community agree with one another. It is necessary that they communicate with one another, for the basis of community is communication. In order to communicate with one another, the members of the community must understand one another, and this means that they must have a common language and a common stock of ideas. Any system of education that is based on the training of individual differences is fraudulent in this sense. The primary object of education should be to bring out our common humanity. For though men are different, they are also the same, and their common humanity, rather than their individual differences, requires development today as at no earlier era in history.

How, then, can higher education escape dogmatism, narrowness, the invasion of academic freedom, and failure in its proper intellectual task and still do its duty by morals and religion? A possible answer lies in the Great Conversation. The Great Conversation began with the Greeks, the Hebrews, the

Hindus, and the Chinese and has continued to the present day. It is a conversation that deals, perhaps more extensively than it deals with anything else, with morals and religion. The questions of the nature and existence of God, the nature and destiny of man, and the organization and purpose of human society are the recurring themes of the Great Conversation.

There may be many ways in which a college or university can continue the Great Conversation, but it would seem off-hand that one of the best ways is through the reading and discussion by all the students of the books in which the Great Conversation has been carried on by the greatest men who have taken part in it. I emphasize discussion because of the contributions that this method makes to the moral and intellectual habits we desire; and I emphasize reading and discussion by all the students and faculty because in this way the formation of a community can be advanced. To continue and enrich the Great Conversation is the object of higher education.

The Civilization of the Dialogue is the only civilization worth having and the only civilization in which the whole world can unite. It is, therefore, the only civilization we can hope for, because the world must unite or be blown to bits. The Civilization of the Dialogue requires communication. It requires a common language and a common stock of ideas. It assumes that every man has reason and that every man can use it. It preserves to every man his independent judgment and, since it does so, it deprives any man or any group of men of the privilege of forcing their judgment upon any other man or group of men. The Civilization of the Dialogue is the negation of force. We have reached the point, in any event, when force cannot unite the world; it can merely destroy it. Through continuing and enriching the Great Conversation higher education not only does its duty by morals and religion; it not only performs its proper intellectual task: it also supports and symbolizes the highest hopes and the highest aspirations of mankind.

October 24, 1948

THREE

THE DEMOCRATIC DILEMMA

1: THE DOCTRINE OF ADAPTATION

The philosophy of education, by which I mean a reasoned and coherent statement of its aims and possibilities, is a secondary subject, dependent on our conception of man and society, that is, upon our philosophy in general. The chaos now obtaining in the philosophy of education results from the chaos in philosophy in general.

In order to demonstrate the existence of this chaos, we will first examine the prevailing theories or doctrines of education, indicating the consequences that each has had, or is likely to have, upon the progress of mankind. These theories or doctrines I take to be the doctrine of adaptation or adjustment; the doctrine of immediate needs, or what might be called the doctrine of the *ad hoc;* the doctrine of social reform; and the doctrine that we need no doctrine at all. I shall then attempt to outline a doctrine that seems, because it is based upon a sounder philosophy in general, to offer more hope as a philosophy of education.

The examples I shall use are largely American. The principal reason for this is, of course, that I have spent thirty years as a teacher and administrator in American educational institutions. But there are other reasons, too. America is a sign and a portent. American technology, which has been a most significant force in moulding American society, seems destined to extend throughout the world. America was the first country to try to educate a whole population, and, as other countries take up this program, as they seem sure to do, they are likely to encounter some of the same problems with which America is now wrestling. America has suddenly emerged as the richest and most powerful nation in the world. Since every nation wants to be rich and powerful, it is possible that many—and there are signs of this already—will feel that one way to become rich and powerful is to imitate the American educational system. It may be useful to raise the question whether America has become rich and powerful because of her educational system or in spite of it. Finally, the decay of philosophy has taken place on a world-wide scale; but the effects of this decay on education have for many reasons been more immediate and more pronounced in America than anywhere else. By observing the effects of the decay of philosophy on education in America, the European may, perhaps, learn what is in store for education throughout the world.

Every ambition, at least every formal, material, institutional ambition, of the reformers, philanthropists, and optimists of the nineteenth century has now been achieved. They wanted to end slavery, lengthen life, raise the standard of living, establish universal free education, and create one world. Science and technology were to be the principal instruments by which happiness and prosperity were to be forged. Science and technology have performed nobly. But the optimism is gone.

Thirty-five years ago we could sing with Shelley:

> The world's great age begins anew
> The golden years return
> And earth doth like a snake renew
> Her winter weeds outworn.
> Heaven smiles: and faiths and empires gleam
> Like wrecks of a dissolving dream.

Now we question whether legal slavery is the only slavery there is, whether a longer life is necessarily a good thing if that life is aimless, whether improvement in the material conditions of existence can solve the fundamental problems of existence, whether one bad world may not be worse than many, and whether science and technology can give us the wisdom to use the power they have brought us for the benefit rather than the destruction of mankind. We question particularly whether universal compulsory free education is, as we always supposed it was, a sufficient method of dealing with all the issues raised by freeing the slaves, giving everybody the vote, and developing industrialism.

The Enlightenment based its hopes of progress on the spread of universal education; and one of its children, Edward Gibbon, in his celebrated chapter summarizing the reasons for the fall of the Western Empire, relieves the fears of Europe by saying that there never will be another barbarian conqueror. His reason is simple. War now requires the knowledge of a large number of arts and sciences. Hence to excel in war the barbarian must cease to be barbarous. Since man first discovered how to master the forces of nature all history has been tending toward this goal. Gibbon's final remark is, "We may therefore acquiesce in the pleasing conclusion that every age of the world has increased and still increases the real wealth, the happiness, the knowledge, and perhaps the virtue of the human race."

The conclusion is pleasing, but seems to be false. There is evidence that the rate of increase in real wealth is declining and none that the happiness and virtue of the human race are increasing. And we know now that a conqueror equipped with knowledge can be more barbarous, as well as more dangerous, than any of his unlettered predecessors.

Now we are told that education, which was to give us political equality and justice, has actually increased the power of the ruling oligarchies at the expense of the masses; and at the same time we are informed that our only hope in combating public and private propaganda lies in raising the level of mass cultivation. This will make the masses propaganda proof.

Victor Ratner, once vice-president of the Columbia Broadcasting System, says, "Radio is made in the image of the American people. To lambaste it is itself un-American. The critics hit at it because they claim to be shocked at what the United States' people are. Radio fits the people. The masses like comic books, Betty Grable, broad comedy, simple drama —it's vulgar, fast, simple, fundamental. Critics of radio often speak about the people's fare; yet they seem to refuse to face the facts about the people's taste. Such criticisms are really criticisms of the American educational system for not raising the cultural level of Americans; for not getting them interested in the better things when they are young. Radio then gets the blame for this failure."

The proposal is to remake the public, to fend off the influences of the media of mass communication, by raising the level of mass cultivation through the system of universal compulsory education.

This leads first to the very large question whether and to what extent the state of mind of the public is or can be the result of its educational system. Universal free compulsory education would seem to be a reflection of what the country wants. One of the most important ideas about education is compressed into the Platonic line: "What is honored in a country will be cultivated there." This is true at the highest levels, in determining the course of research and advanced study. The interest in science and technology in the United States today must result from the honor in which scientists and technologists are held and from the high value that is set upon their work. It is even truer at the level of universal compulsory education, because the object of the system must be to make the children as far as possible what their parents or the ruling group in the community want the next generation to be. This is what will be honored in the country. It does not seem an exaggeration to say that a system of universal free compulsory education, however expensive or prolonged, can do no more than try to give the people what they want already. It cannot make them want something different. If the American people honored wisdom and goodness as they now honor power and success, the system of universal free education would be quite different from what it is today. But how can the system of universal free education, which is busily cultivating what the people now honor, teach them to honor something else?

This would seem to be a sufficient answer to Mr. Ratner. But there are other answers, too. As the arrangements in other parts of the world show, there is no inherent reason why the American radio should be conducted for profit; and there is no reason why it should be conducted as it is, even if it is conducted for profit. To give all the best time to vaudeville and all the rest to soap opera is a crime for which the fine music that comes occasionally over the air cannot atone. Why should Mr. Ratner demand that the educational system do for him something he could at least in part achieve himself? A man who has a monopoly, and then sells shoddy merchandise, can hardly blame the low taste of the public or the ineffectiveness of its educational system for his prosperity. The public has nowhere to turn. Mr. Ratner has no monopoly; but he and his colleagues in other broadcasting companies are so busy imitating one another that what the listener finds on one station he will find on another; and, if he does not like what he finds, he must turn his radio off altogether.

The final answer is that from the standpoint of time alone the proposal places an undue burden on the schools. As Alfred North Whitehead remarked, "The whole problem of education is controlled by lack of time. If Methuselah was not educated, it was his own fault or that of his teachers." A child is in school for only a small portion of his life, and even when he is of school age he is not protected, after hours, from the terrific storm of propaganda that now beats upon the citizen. The notion that the child can be inoculated against propaganda once and for all in childhood seems naive. It is hardly possible that this task can be accomplished for life in eight, twelve, or sixteen years.

Nevertheless we must admit that the sort of popular education now prevalent in America, and destined, I believe, to spread over the West, has not raised the level of mass cultivation.

How do you get a country to want to raise the level of mass cultivation? This depends on criticism, criticism by individuals, minorities, and centers of independent thought. This is the reason for academic freedom and freedom of speech generally. The best definition of a university that I have been able to think of is that it is a center of independent thought. It may be a good many other things as well; but, if it is not this, it has failed. The principal function of a professional school in a university is not to train men for the profession, but to criticize the profession. Unless criticism of the culture is permitted, the culture cannot be changed; certainly the schools will not be permitted to change it.

How do you get a country to permit criticism? This can only be done if the country recognizes that an uncriticized culture cannot long endure. The hope of the West is that the church and the university are still free. I must add that there is no hope in the university unless it takes seriously its mission as a center of independent thought.

But in the West, where the chance still exists, little effort is made to raise the level of mass cultivation through the schools. The leading theories or doctrines of education say nothing on this subject.

The first of these is the theory of adjustment. Here the object is to fit the student into his physical, social, political, economic, and intellectual environment with a minimum of discomfort to the society. Freud took the view that the object of education was to make young people healthy and efficient, to adapt them to their surroundings, to make them successful in the terms of the society in which they were brought up. His summary is: "I should go so far as to say that revolutionary children are not desirable from any point of view." This caution seems unnecessary; for no society would tolerate a revolutionary educational system.

So T. S. Eliot seems to give his powerful sanction to an educational program that adapts the child to the political organization under which he is to live.

So the chief aim of UNESCO in fundamental education, which is the principal program of the organization, is to enable the peoples of underdeveloped countries "to adjust themselves to their changing environment."

In America the doctrine of adjustment is perhaps the leading theory. Here it results from a misconception of John Dewey. Since he is a very bad writer, his followers may be excused for their failure to notice that when he talked about adjusting to the environment, he meant that the environment should first be improved. Dewey was essentially a social reformer, and it is tragic that he should have laid the foundation for the proposition that the aim of education is to adjust the young to their environment, good or bad.

The theory of adjustment leads to a curriculum of miscellaneous dead facts. The way to adjust to the environment is to learn the facts about the environment. Since it is impossible to tell what the environment will be, the student can only be informed about the environment that exists while he is in school. But all that is known with certainty about the environment is that it will be different by the time the student has to adjust to it.

The doctrine of adjustment or adaptation is not well adapted to America. America is, and always has been, a society in transition. Seventy million Americans live in a different house today from the one they occupied ten years ago. America is the example par excellence of the rapidity of technological change. Vocations employing thousands of men may be wiped out over night and be replaced by others that were not thought of the day before.

One of the most popular courses in the American schools is stenography. Think of the havoc that will be wrought if the dictating machine becomes the standard method of conducting office correspondence. A great American university has established a school of what is called cosmetology, announcing that what it called the profession of beautician "is the fastest growing in this state." Think what will happen to the graduates of this educational institution if self-beautification for ladies becomes as simple a matter as it is for men.

America is probably the easiest place to earn a living in the world. Yet more emphasis is placed on vocational training in the American schools than in any others. There are many reasons for this that will appear in the course of these lectures; but the one I wish to mention now is the result of the proposition that what is honored in a country will be cultivated there. We must admit that what is honored in America is material success. All you have to do to understand this is to compare the position of intellectuals and artists in

America with their position in Europe. The model American is the successful businessman. Artists and intellectuals are regarded in the light of charity patients or excess baggage. Consequently the attention of the American is drawn at an early date to the necessity of adjusting himself to his economic environment in such a way that he will be successful.

I shall attempt in a moment a general critique of the doctrine of adjustment or adaptation. Here I wish to mention one or two consequences of that branch of the doctrine which deals with economic or vocational adjustment. The question it raises is this: assuming that the young must adjust to their enviroment, including their economic environment, can the educational system manage, supervise, and direct the whole job? In particular can the educational system give a boy as good a training for a particular task in industry as the industry itself could give him? In America technical institutes of the European type are virtually unknown. Vocational training is given along with all other types of training in the same schools. Because of the relative ease of vocational instruction and because of the immediate interest it excites on the part of the pupil, such instruction has the tendency to force out of the course of study any other kind of instruction. Yet we learned in the war that the airplane companies could produce in a few weeks better airplane mechanics than the schools could produce in years. The pupils in the schools were necessarily trained by obsolescent teachers with obsolescent machinery. Hence the result of the emphasis on vocational training in America is poor mechanics without education.

America is not only the easiest place to earn a living in the world; it is also the place with the most leisure in the world. The average industrial worker in America gets more than fifty dollars for a forty-hour week. He now works twenty hours a week less than he did forty years ago. At the same time that industrial operations have been simplified to the point where little or no training is required for them—they can in fact be performed by twelve-year-old children—unprecedented leisure has opened before the American citizen. Still one of the principal aims of the educational system is to educate the citizen to work for a living. It does not educate him in the right use of his leisure.

The new found leisure of the American is therefore spent in relaxation, and that provided by the tavern and the television set is almost equally demoralizing. The twin aims that have animated mankind since the dawn of history, the conquest of nature and relief from drudgery, now almost accomplished in America, have ended in the trivialization of our lives.

There are, of course, many reasons for this; but one of them surely is that our educational system has given us no resources that we can employ to give our leisure time significance. When we are not working, all we can do is to amuse ourselves. The deep and permanent melancholia that underlies the American temperament must be ascribed, in part at least, to the boredom that the perpetual search for amusement at length induces.

Let us remember that Socrates and Gandhi did not seek to adapt themselves to society as they found it. They attempted to re-make society, and the fact that they died in the attempt in no way detracts from their glory or from their value as examples to other men. To Freud we may oppose Kant, who said, "Parents usually educate their children merely in such a manner that, however bad the world may be, they may adapt themselves to its present conditions." This may suggest to us that the doctrine of adaptation is not so new as its proponents would have us believe. Kant goes on: "But they ought to give them an education so much better than this, that a better condition of things may thereby be brought about in the future."

The pressure in America, especially intense now in this period of the cold war, is toward an unwavering conformity of life and thought. University professors are being required in some states to take special oaths attesting that they have never been members of the Communist party, and this in spite of the fact that, unless a recent ambiguous decision of the Supreme Court has changed the law, it is perfectly legal to be a Communist in the United States. The irresponsible fulminations of Senator McCarthy strike terror into the hearts of innocent government employees.[1] Students who exhibit the slightest variation from established fashions of thought and action ask me whether they are neurotic. And, in fact, I attribute the popularity of psychoanalysis in the United States in a large part to the prevailing impression that everybody who is not just like everybody else, or, worse still, who does not want to be, must be sick.

At least during a cold war, the doctrine of adaptation leads remorselessly to indoctrination. I will read you a few exemplary passages from a letter addressed to all the teachers in a Middle Western city by the superintendent of schools, who, under the law of the state, has the power to oust any of them from their jobs. The superintendent says, "The threat to American institutions by international Communism makes imperative that greater emphasis be given in our schools to the study of the meaning, significance, and the value of American Democracy. Indoctrination has never been in good repute among educators in the United States . . . It now appears necessary for the schools in the United States to indoctrinate American youth for American Democracy . . . In our present confused world, it is essential in America that we teach our young people that American Democracy is the best government in the world and that we explain why it is the best . . . They must understand that American Democracy was founded on private enterprise and that this economic system has brought forth a great and powerful nation which will continue to grow even stronger by perpetuating and protecting private enterprise." And so on.

Although I believe that democracy is the best form of government, that the American democracy is a very good form of democracy, and that the economic system known as private enterprise has made significant contributions to the development of my country, I ask myself whether it is possible for the American democracy to be improved and whether the American system of private enterprise has no defects, and also whether pupils who have been indoctrinated as this superintendent proposes can be expected to take an active part in improving the American government or remedying the defects of the American economic system. I also feel some sympathy for the confusion and disappointment that these pupils will experience when they emerge from the dream world of indoctrination and face the facts of life.

Here we see the doctrine of adaptation reduced to an absurdity; for the passion to adjust the young to the environment has so carried away this superintendent that in the name of adjustment he proposes to adjust the young, not to the environment, but to his conception of the environment, which can only result in maladjusting them to the environment as it actually is.

We hear during the cold war in America that the American way of life is in danger. You would suppose, to listen to the people who say this, that the American way of life consisted in unanimous tribal apotheosis. Yet the history and tradition of our country make it plain that the essence of the American way of life is its hospitality to criticism, protest, unpopular opinions, and independent thought. The great American word has always been freedom, and, in particular, freedom of thought, speech, and assembly. Asserting the dignity of man, and of every man, America has proclaimed and protected the freedom to differ. America has grown strong on criticism. It would be quite as consistent with the American way of life to offer prizes for the most penetrating criticism of our country as it would be to offer prizes to those who have done the best job of advertising it. The heart of democracy is independent criticism; the basic freedom is freedom of thought and expression.

Non-legal methods of persecuting people into conformity are steadily gaining popularity in the West. Such methods are little better than purges and pogroms. The ideas to which the West, and a large part of the East, are most bitterly opposed are the police state, the abolition of freedom of speech, thought, and association, and the notion that the individual exists for the state. Yet in practice there may not be a significant difference between a society in which such compulsions are exerted by the tyrannical power of the state or by the tyrannical power of public opinion.

The doctrine of adjustment or adaptation explicitly excludes any consideration of standards. The adjustment must take place, whether the environment is good or bad. An educational system that is based on this theory must, therefore, ultimately become a system without values.

2: THE DOCTRINE OF IMMEDIATE NEEDS

The doctrine of immediate needs, or the doctrine of the *ad hoc,* looks, in terms of its practical results, a good deal like the doctrine of adaptation or adjustment to the environment. The course of study in the woman's college that I described to you previously, where the curriculum is based on the diaries of 323 mature women, could be justified either on the ground that this program of study would adapt the graduates of the college to a society where mature women were behaving in this way or on the ground that young women needed to learn to behave in this way in order to behave like mature women.

Or take an announcement made not long ago in an educational journal in America on behalf of the high school of San Diego, California. It states that the high school has extended its requirements for graduation beyond the usual academic hurdles and now includes in these requirements what are called "Essentials for Effective Living." Among the essentials for effective living appear the following: ability to apply first aid; ability to take care of one's self in the water (we are reminded that San Diego is a seaport town); ability to engage in two or three sports that may carry over into adult life; ability to write business letters; ability to fill out application blanks; and ability to budget one's income. The girls have to acquire in addition ability to buy the right kind of food and prepare it; ability to choose the right kind of clothes and take care of them; ability to take care of a home; and ability to take care of children. The boys must acquire ability to use and take care of simple tools, ability to make minor repairs on household plumbing, ability to repair simple electrical equipment, and ability to repair furniture. All are required to learn how to keep clean and neat and use good manners.

Miss Elsa Bauer, chairman of the committee that made the announcement, said, "These embrace the skills and information necessary to be a good citizen, to earn an adequate living, to make a good home, and to maintain good health and contentment." Miss Bauer adds, "For some of the skills designated, the paper-and-pencil test is of questionable value. For these will be substituted statements from authorized persons, such as life guards, YMCA directors, and other responsible adults."

You will notice that the object of this interesting educational program is to supply the skills and information necessary to be a good citizen, to earn an adequate living, to make a good home, and to maintain good health and contentment. An educational system that can accomplish these things, and accomplish them in one course, has reason to be proud of itself. The assumption is that if you can take care of yourself in the water, provided you live in a seaport town, if you can fill out application blanks, and make minor repairs on household plumbing, together with a few other matters of similar intellectual significance, you will at one stroke have adapted yourself to society and met all your human needs.

The doctrine of immediate needs, or the doctrine of the *ad hoc,* rests on the proposition that individuals need to be able to do things in order to succeed in the current definition of success and that societies need to have things done in order to be more successful in the same definition. Individuals and societies need useful things; most of these things are material goods and services.

Hear Harold Benjamin, dean of education at the University of Maryland. He says, "Too long Latin has been considered general education and driving a car as special or vocational training. Exactly the reverse is true. Latin is useful only to those students whose needs and abilities require it, while driving a car is useful to everybody." Mr. Benjamin goes on to say that what happened to France after 1939 was a devastating commentary on the French *lycée,* thus intimating that, if the *lycée* had offered instruction in automobile driving, the course of history might have been different and that, unless America takes warning by the fate of France and introduces such instruction at once, she may be overtaken by the same fate.

The reverse of this moving appeal by Mr. Benjamin is the story of that Dean of Christ Church who was asked by a student what was the use of studying Greek. The Dean replied, "It is not only the immediate language of the Holy Ghost, but it leads to positions of great dignity and emolument."

In so far as the woman's college mentioned, the San Diego High School, Mr. Benjamin, and the Dean of Christ Church are concerned with the needs of students—to behave like mature women, to understand household plumbing, to drive a car, and to achieve positions of dignity and emolument— they are all wrong, though for different reasons. If we can ever find out what the educational system should do, I am sure we shall discover that it will be so difficult as to demand all the time and attention we can give it. It follows that whatever can be learned outside the educational system should be learned outside it, because the educational system has enough to do teaching what can be learned only in the system. The words of Sir Richard Livingstone should be written in letters of fire on every schoolroom wall: "The good schoolmaster is known by the number of valuable subjects he declines to teach." Even if driving a car, understanding plumbing, and behaving like a mature woman are valuable subjects, they can be, and therefore should be, learned outside the educational system.

The study of Greek no longer leads to any positions except positions in the teaching of Greek, which, though of great dignity, are not of great emolument. As identifying a need on the part of the student does not identify a necessity in the curriculum, so identifying a need at one time gives us no assurance that it will continue. If either automobile driving or Greek is to be made a part of the course of study, the argument must rest on something more than that it is or was a need. There are too many needs, too many evanescent needs, too many needs that the educational system cannot effectively cope with.

To refer once more to my favorite woman's college, the President told me that it would consume twenty-five years of a student's time to study all the courses offered at his institution. This will suggest the unlimited possibilities of an educational program based on the needs of students. It will also reveal the pitiful plight of the girls, who, on completing their work at this college at the end of two years, must feel that twenty-three twenty-fifths of their needs remain unmet. It seems altogether likely that in this case, as in many others, the college decided that the more courses it could offer, the more students it could attract.

One trouble with the doctrine of needs is the difficulty of identifying a need. How do you know a need when you see one? The usual answer is that you know one by the demand. And the next step is to enlarge your market by the best advertising and sales techniques through creating a demand for something you could offer to meet it. Since the public is likely to have a greater appetite for the *ad hoc,* which can be easily understood, and which, it is hoped, will have immediate practical results, than it has for serious learning, educational institutions that want public support, as all educational institutions in America do, will constantly expand their *ad hoc* activities.

The doctrine of needs thus ends in public relations. I think it fair to say that the dominant concern of school superintendents and university presidents in America is public relations. I have no doubt that the superintendent whose letter I read to you urged indoctrination in the American way of life with a view to ingratiating the school system with the taxpayers, so that, when his plans or expenditures came up for public discussion, he could avail himself of the popularity that his staunch Americanism had won for him. There is not a college or university president in America who would not get rid of what is called big-time intercollegiate football if he felt that it was safe to do so. The howls of the alumni and the public, who have come to rely on his institution to supply them with entertainment on Saturday afternoons in the autumn, ring in his ears as he considers such a decision, and he concludes that it would not be safe.

You know, then, that something is a need because somebody wants it. If the group that wants it is powerful enough, either by reason of its influence or its numbers, to affect your public standing adversely if you do not do what it wants, you do what it wants. Or you try, or, if necessary, pretend, to do what it wants. For many things people want the educational system to do for them it cannot do.

A special problem is created for the American university by the characteristic social, political, and economic organizations of the country, which are known as pressure groups. They have, many of them, the most laudable objects; but their principal object is to get something done. They constantly think of the educational system, and in particular of the universities, as the means through which they can accomplish their desires.

If an occupational group, like the beauticians, for example, wants to combine the high purpose of raising the standards of the occupation with the somewhat different purpose of restricting competition, it will naturally occur to them that the creation of a school for beauticians in the state university, through which all prospective competitors must pass, will limit the number of prospective competitors and enhance the dignity and standing of the occupation. Since almost all occupations in America are organized in this way, and since they all have the same ambitions, there is no end to the creation of new professional schools, as they are euphemistically called, in the American universities.

The American universities, because of the influence that these groups may have upon the legislatures that support the state institutions or because of the role that they may be expected to play as donors or fee payers to the private universities, have been unable to resist the claims of these occupational groups. Nor are they able to resist the appeals of industry. The vice-president of a great textile house once described to me his efforts to get some chemical research done by a university department. It was work on a trade secret. He investigated the departments of two or three institutions, only to find that they were allied with his competitors. He finally found a chemistry department in a respectable university that was willing to turn the entire attention of its staff to his problems and not to tell anybody but him the results. "Think of it," he said; "they were willing to do this for $20,000 a year."

Of course, one reason why this chemistry department was willing to do this was that it was not very good. The professors were not intelligent enough to have any problems of their own. But I think the basic reason lies deeper: the Amercian university is supposed to assist in the solution of any current practical problem that anybody has. And when there is money in it, and good public relations in it, the fact that the project runs counter to the purpose of the university, which is to pursue knowledge for its own sake, does not make the lure of such work any easier to resist. The purpose of the university has long since been changed; it is now regarded as a service station for the community. So far have we come from the conception of a university as a center of independent thought.

Let us turn to the basic consequences of the doctrine of needs in education in the West.

One thing, we are told, the democratic citizen in the modern world needs first of all, and that is information. He must have information on every conceivable subject, because his duties as a citizen require him to pass on every conceivable subject. He lives in a world that is being re-made by science and technology. He must know all about them. In America we are reminded that our people have only lately emerged from their isolation to assume a position of world leadership. Americans should know all about Europe, and all about Africa, and all about the Near, Middle, and Far East, as well. Americans should know all about everything.

The first difficulty with this proposition is that current needs and current information simply will not stay current. The rapidity of change in every field today is such that what the father knows of the facts of life is almost useless to his son. Those who painfully acquired information about the Weimar Republic or the Chinese Empire in response to felt needs can feel little need of it now.

The second difficulty with the proposition that everybody

has to know all the facts about everything is that there are too many facts. So one of the most eminent sociologists in America reached the conclusion a few years ago that there were now so many facts that everybody ought to know that in order to get time to pour all the facts into the young we should have to prolong adolescence at least until age 45. We had, in short, to make a new definition of youth so that people might learn everything while young.

A final difficulty with the proposition that everybody ought to know all the facts about everything is that it tends to produce an educational program that is upsidedown. If you are going to pour all the facts about the world into the young, you have to start early. Yet the one conclusion of Aristotle with which all educators must agree is that children cannot deal with the facts of the world about them. Aristotle concluded that in order to understand the facts of life you have to have experience; these facts cannot be comprehended by the inexperienced. History, literature, moral and political philosophy, and the social sciences will not yield up their full lessons to the immature.

In a country where the people continue their education through their adult lives this difficulty is troublesome enough. Where there is no serious program of adult education, it takes on more menacing proportions. There the proposition that everybody must learn all about everything means that everybody must learn all about everything while he is in school. The inevitable result is that the course of study is jammed with every conceivable subject on the ground that the pupil might find that he needed to know about it, or society might need to have him know about it, in his adult life. The subjects are so numerous that the pupil leaves school without having mastered any of them.

As the doctrine of needs, or of the *ad hoc*, has promoted the disintegration of the program of the schools, so it has promoted the disintegration of the universities. One thing we are all certain of is that society needs specialists and that a man needs to be a specialist if he is to have a successful career. In countries where there is a good basic education this creates no significant problem. The intellectual community rests on this basic education, and specialists can communicate with one other because of the common language, the common stock of ideas, and the common tradition that this basic education has given them. The university of Imperial Germany was an aggregation of specialists. But it would not have been educationally successful or socially tolerable without the humanistic *gymnasium*.

The American university as we know it today was founded by men who had studied in Germany and who sought, in the last decades of the last century, to establish the German university in the United States. But they did not import the humanistic *gymnasium*. On the contrary, their efforts to build up universities on the German model in the United States succeeded just as the American high school and the American college were beginning to fall apart under the strain imposed upon them by the huge numbers that flocked to them as the twentieth century opened.

The tremendous success, in material, practical terms, that specialism instantly achieved in America led to greater and greater fragmentation of knowledge, with specialists operating in small parts of each fragment. We have now reached the situation where the work of a man in one part of a fragment is incomprehensible to one in another part of the same fragment, to say nothing of a man in another subject. The unity of the modern American university is therefore only geographical, and the topics that can be discussed at the faculty club are the weather and politics, for these are the only subjects the members have in common. When I was on the faculty of Yale, we did not teach English in the Engineering School; we taught Engineering English. This meant, of course, that an engineer was taught to talk only to another engineer. Since fifty per cent of the graduates of the Engineering School did not become engineers, I can only assume that they went through life cut off from communication with their fellow countrymen.

All this has had a curious effect on college education in America, which a man begins normally at 18 and completes with the bachelor's degree at 22. It is possible for a boy to receive this degree in many state universities after studying two years of military training, two years of German, physics, chemistry, mathematics, and nothing else. But the inadequacy of his preliminary training and the low standards that he has to meet mean not that he has been well trained in physics, chemistry, mathematics, and German, but that he has not been trained in anything else. Whereas specialization purports to give intensified education in the subject matter of the specialty, what it actually does is to inhibit education outside the specialty.[2]

At the beginning of this century every graduate of a French *lycée* or a German *gymnasium* or an Italian *liceo* had acquired at the close of 12 years of schooling, at about 18 years of age, approximately as much knowledge of subject matter as three modern college graduates together will have acquired in the United States after 16 years of schooling, at about age 22. If a college student in America specializes in mathematics, he will have arrived at the age of 22 at such branches as differential and integral calculus, analytical geometry, and differential equations. The fundamentals of most of these fields were, however, known to 18-year-old graduates of the old-fashioned European secondary schools, who also knew equally well three other subjects at least: Latin, Greek, and their native tongue.

If a modern American student is graduated from college as a specialist in classical languages at 22, he will not have reached the level that a pupil of an Italian *liceo* had to reach at about 17. The Italian pupil had to be able by that time to make public, extemporaneous discourses in Latin and to participate in public debates in Latin. And we must remember that these Italian schoolboys knew the calculus as well.

The process of specialization has therefore turned out to be a process of inhibition. The traditional definition of a specialist is that he is a man who learns more and more about less and less. In the United States we have discovered that he can be a man who learns less and less about less and less.

These differences between the intellectual accomplishments of American and European students are everywhere admitted in the United States. It is denied, however, that they result from any failure on the part of the American educational system. It is said, first, that America aims to educate everybody, whereas Europe aims to educate the few. It is unfair to compare the attainments of the mass with those of the elite.

It is true that America has up to now undertaken to educate a larger proportion of its youth than any other country in the West. In England today 32% of the children of 14 or over are in school. In the United States the proportion is 76%. In England 20,000 students will enter institutions of higher learning next autumn. In the United States the number is 600,000. We have five times the population and thirty times the number of students above the secondary schools. The difficulties created by the sheer quantity of the American educational enterprise are doubtless very great. Think of the number of teachers that is required. And with that amiable spirit of contradiction characteristic of the Anglo-Saxon race, Americans, who are devoted to education, refuse to pay living wages to their school teachers. The estimate is that 300,000 teachers will quit the profession in the next three years, of whom we shall lose 125,000 this year, not counting those who will die, marry, or retire on account of age. And ten million more children that are at present in school are expected to enroll by 1960.

The second American comment on the difference between the attainments of American and European students is that the attainments of European students, though interesting, are incomplete, and incomplete in the most important respects. What good does it do the Italian student to be able to make an extemporaneous address in Latin, when he will never feel the need of making one in later life, and would probably not be allowed to make one if he did? What good does it do the graduate of the *lycée* to know the calculus, if he does not know how to take care of his teeth? What can we expect of a continent in which the young have never been taught how to apply first aid, take care of themselves in the water, engage in two or three sports that may carry over into adult life, write business letters, fill out application blanks, or budget their incomes, to say nothing of making minor repairs on household plumbing? No wonder Europe is impoverished and decadent and America is rich and powerful.

An American concerned about his country, concerned that her riches and power may be a boon and not a danger to mankind, may however inquire if it is altogether clear that the relative poverty and weakness of Europe can result entirely from the intellectual superiority of its educational system. He may ask whether the huge internal market, the absence of political subdivisions, the use of a common language, the tremendous natural resources, and the hitherto impregnable position of America may not have had as much to do with the power and riches of the country as the unusual character of American education. He may even ask whether it would have been possible for a country less rich and powerful than America to survive the educational system that she has.

Such an American may ask, too, whether keeping everybody in school longer than any other country necessarily means that everybody in America is better educated than the mass of the population in any other country. He may ask whether the American educational system actually does adjust the young to their environment or meet the needs of the individual and of society. In particular he may be permitted to doubt whether the effort to fit the young into their current surroundings and to teach them to solve current problems will equip them with that intellectual power which will enable them to meet new situations and solve new problems as they arise. It would appear that with the extraordinary fluidity of American society and the drastic changes that have occurred and are occurring in America's relations with the rest of the world the intellectual powers that go by the name of understanding and judgment are the prime requisite of the American citizen.

Perhaps the greatest idea that America has given the world is the idea of education for all. The world is entitled to know whether this idea means that everybody can be educated, or only that everybody must go to school. If education is to be nothing but a housing project, then we can understand why the hopes the nineteenth century had of it have not been fulfilled: the nineteenth century was afflicted with a delusion; it was off in pursuit of an impractical ideal. If the education of the whole population is impossible, the sooner we abandon the idea the better.

To these questions, what education is and who can and should be educated, I shall revert at a later time. But I cannot conclude this discussion of the doctrine of needs, or of the *ad hoc*, without indicating its significance for the majority of the population of the world today. They are the peoples of the so-called underdeveloped countries. They are lacking in what the West regards as the indispensable requirements of life, not of civilized life, but of life itself. Their needs are great and pitiful; they need everything. First of all they need useful things, material goods and services.

It is now widely believed that the West should help them get these things, and with this conclusion anybody with a spark of human feeling must agree. At the same time the question arises whether helping them get these things, and doing nothing more, will have the results that are universally anticipated. The general expectation is that, if they have food, clothing, shelter, and adequate sanitation and are assisted on the road to industrialization, they will be happy, or at least happier than they were before. In America it is felt that if they have these things they will line up on the side of the West in the cold war.

In the first place, this theory seems to come close to the Marxian fallacy that the character and conduct of men are determined by the conditions of production. Nothing in history suggests that prosperous nations are less warlike than impoverished ones. Nothing suggests that industrialized countries are less revolutionary than agricultural ones. The people of underdeveloped countries need material goods because they are unable to realize their potentialities as men at their present level of life. We should help them for this reason and not because we expect them to behave as we would like them to behave.

Another Marxian fallacy is that when the economic problem has been solved, when the classless society has been achieved, peace will reign and men will change from voracious animals into angels. All experience with classless societies, such as universities and monasteries, where the economic differences among the members are slight and no one is exploiting anybody else in the Marxian sense, shows that Marx's expectations of peace in the classless society were bound to be disappointed. I can testify that the university, at least, is constantly torn by internecine feuds of the bitterest intensity.

Supplying the peoples of underdeveloped countries with the means of economic development is a much more complicated subject than is commonly assumed. Recent reports on cotton farming in Syria show that the result of mechanization in this field is that the rich are getting richer and the poor poorer. The reason of course is that only the rich can afford the expensive equipment that large-scale irrigation demands. If we are going to be of real help to underdeveloped countries, something beyond material assistance is needed, principally a sense of what a just society is and a willingness to face the disagreeable consequences of joining with the downtrodden to obtain justice for them at the hands of the dominant members of the community. The billions wasted in China should warn us of the consequences of assisting the corrupt rulers of an unjust society.

The industrial revolution in Japan occurred overnight. Much help came from the West to make the change possible. Educational advisers went out from America. The ruling classes of Japan absorbed the technology of the West to become richer, more powerful, and more bellicose than they had been before. The common people became poorer, weaker, and more insignificant than ever. The two great convictions of modern man, that all problems can be solved by production and education, were shown once more to be illusions. We saw again that production can increase poverty and that education can increase ignorance. The case of the much-vaunted literacy of the Japanese provides striking confirmation of the conclusions of Toynbee and Huxley that the spread of universal, free, compulsory education has promoted the degradation and enslavement of men.

The education that is now proposed for underdeveloped

countries, apart from technical training, looks toward the abolition of illiteracy. But of course the question is, what will illiterates read when they have become literate? Do we know it would be an advantage to have people able to read *Mein Kampf*, if they read nothing but *Mein Kampf*? Are we even sure that it is an advantage to have young people able to read comic books, which I take to be the principal cultural manifestation in America in our time?

We cannot even be certain that extensive schooling will actually wipe out illiteracy. The high literacy rate of the Japanese was largely a fiction, and it has been estimated that 50% of the male population of the Chicago high schools are functionally illiterate, that is, they can read letters, or even words; but they cannot tell you what they mean. At best, literacy is a power like any other. It is neutral, like atomic energy; it can be used for evil as well as good. To assume that everybody will be peaceful and happy if everybody has gone to school or learned to read is as foolish as it is to assume that everybody will be peaceful and happy if the world is industrialized.

I am in favor of material goods, which are undoubtedly goods, of literacy, schooling, and even, within limits, of industrialization. I merely point out that if, in dealing with underdeveloped countries, we are so carried away by the doctrine of immediate needs, the doctrine of the *ad hoc,* that we look only to these immediate needs, the last state of the underdeveloped countries and of the world will be no better, and may well be worse, than the first. The problem is how to help these countries meet their immediate needs and at the same time lay the foundations for a better society and a better world.

We cannot accomplish this if we look for guidance in education to the doctrine of immediate needs. The needs we are seeking to meet are not immediate. The doctrine of immediate needs provides us with no standards. It gives us no values. It leads us to determine the content of education in terms of the pressures operative in the society. Any connection between these pressures and what is good for the society can at best be coincidental. In the effort to discover how education can help to produce a better society we must turn next to the doctrine of social reform.

3: THE DOCTRINE OF SOCIAL REFORM AND THE DOCTRINE OF NO DOCTRINE AT ALL

Underneath the writings of almost all writers on education lies the doctrine of social reform. They cannot look at the society around them and like it. How is the society to be changed? There are only two ways: revolution and education.

Writers on education are not men of action, still less of blood. They shrink from the havoc of revolution. They dream of carrying through the social changes they desire by means of the peaceful process of instruction.

A brief examination of the case of T. S. Eliot will indicate the pervasiveness of the doctrine of social reform in writings on education and some of the difficulties involved in it. Mr. Eliot's chief complaint of other writers is that they seek to use the schools to achieve the social purposes they have at heart. This, he says, is not education, but something else. Then he falls into the pit he has digged for others; he wants to use the schools to advance social purposes of his own. Mr. Eliot wants a society that has both the class, those who have inherited advantages, and the élite, those who have ability, but who may be without inherited advantages. And so, after anathematizing writers on education who seek to obtain the society they desire through the schools, Mr. Eliot says, "Education should help to preserve the class and select the élite." Since this would be bringing about a social change that Mr. Eliot has at heart, it would not, according to his criticism of others, be education, but something else.

The most influential American writer on education, and the most influential American philosopher, is John Dewey. He remade the American educational system in forty years. He was first of all a social reformer. But his aims were almost exactly opposite to those of Mr. Eliot. He had no objection to the élite; but he was against the class. To him inherited advantages would be unmerited advantages. He was an egalitarian.

These examples raise the first question in regard to the doctrine of social reform, which is this: is it possible to achieve the social purposes one has at heart, is it possible to put over a program of social reform, through the educational system? Every society hopes that its educational system will in some way bring the next generation somewhat closer to achieving some of the society's ideals, those in particular which may be approximated without damage, or with imperceptible damage, to the vested interests in the society, that is, without revolution.

But suppose that the ideals of the social reformer are different from those of the society. When Plato planned his ideal state, he did not propose to start it through education, but to perpetuate it that way. His utopia was to come into being through a miracle, which he properly doubted could ever take place. John Dewey on the other hand succeeded, I think, because the social ideals that he favored were those generally popular in the United States.

It is as unlikely that world government can be presented as a program in the American schools as that Western democracy can be taught as a program in Soviet Russia. A revolution cannot be brought about through the conscious inculcation of revolutionary doctrine in the schools. I am inclined to agree with Mr. Eliot that, if it could be, this would not be education, but something else.

The doctrine of social reform is substantially identical in its results with the doctrine of adaptation and the doctrine of immediate needs. The social reformer is limited to adapting the rising generation to social changes already agreed upon. He is limited to meeting needs that are sanctioned by the society. He can hope to make himself felt in the educational system only after he has won over the society. I should say that at this moment Mr. Eliot, for example, has little chance of persuading the United Kingdom to favor an educational system that preserves the class. It is abolishing the class as rapidly as possible. Unless Mr. Eliot can arouse the population and change the views of those who dominate the United Kingdom, he cannot hope to achieve the social purposes he has at heart through the schools.

Since the doctrine of social reform has the same results as the doctrine of adaptation and the doctrine of immediate needs, the same objections apply to it as apply to the other two.

One in particular needs to be emphasized, and that is the difficulty that grows out of the accomplishment of a program of social reform. Most of the social objects of the organizations devoted to the education of adults in Sweden have now been achieved. What are these organizations to do now? They must either disappear or devote themselves to other purposes. But the problem would be much more acute if Sweden had set itself to attain these goals through the schools. The school system cannot disappear when it has reached its social goals. If intemperance or slums are eliminated, is the school system to go on preaching temperance or the elimination of the slums? If it does, the schools are cluttered with archaic lumber. If it does not, what are the schools to do? If they move on to other social problems, they will have educated one generation to solve problems that no longer exist, and will be educating another to solve those which may not exist when the pupils have left school.

Consider the embarrassment of the movement for the education of adults in England. This movement originated in the demand for social justice, and especially for equality of educational opportunity. Now its objects have been achieved. This is a serious blow to the movement; for it must concede that its aims were too narrow or go out of business. But suppose that this program of social justice had been carried on through the schools. Year after year pupils would have been taught to go out to work for the aims embodied in the Education Act of 1944. How would they feel in 1945? And what would the schools do after 1944?

But I believe that it is dangerous as well as futile to regard the educational system as a means of getting a program of social reform adopted. If one admits the possibility of obtaining through the schools social reforms that one likes, one must also admit the possibility of obtaining social reforms that one dislikes. What happens will depend on the popularity of various reformers, the plausibility of their causes, and the pressure they are able to exert on the educational system.

Am I saying, then, that the educational system cannot participate in the improvement of society? Not at all. I am saying that it is unwise and dangerous to look at the system as Mr. Dewey, and sometimes Mr. Eliot look at it, as an engine of social reform. I take the view that the object of education is the improvement of society. But to make this view effective you have to know what improvement is, and you have to recognize the limitations, as well as the possibilities, of education. Mr. Dewey and Mr. Eliot have a faulty conception of improvement. As a result they have a faulty conception of education. Mr. Dewey has not considered the limitations of education. Mr. Eliot has not adequately considered its possibilities.

The failures of which I think they have been guilty result from the defects of their philosophies. Pragmatism, the philosophy of Dewey and his followers, like positivism, the philosophy of Reichenbach and Carnap, is not a philosophy at all, because it supplies no intelligible standard of good or bad. Pragmatism and positivism hold that the only knowledge is scientific knowledge. As the Mad Hatter and the March Hare in *Alice in Wonderland* celebrated unbirthdays, so pragmatism and positivism are unphilosophies. They are even antiphilosophies. Mr. Eliot's philosophy is more subtle and satisfying and exposes him to less general attack. When he says that education should help to preserve the class and select the élite, when, as in *Notes Towards the Definition of Culture,* he attacks the doctrine of equality of opportunity as the most mistaken and dangerous dogma put forward by writers on education, he errs, but he errs in good company. His views are reminiscent of Aristotle's on the natural slave. But they are wrong nevertheless. They reveal a misconception of the nature of man. Aristotle's views on the natural slave are refuted by a simple reference to his basic proposition that man is a political animal. If all men are men, none of them can by nature be a slave.

These hints may suggest to us the importance of philosophy in general to the philosophy of education, a subject to which we shall return. But let us press on to examine the remaining doctrine that we must review, the doctrine of no doctrine at all.

Thinking is hard work. The development of a coherent

philosophy of education, since it carries us into the formulation of a coherent philosophy in general, is a difficult and ungrateful task. In America the problems presented by getting everybody into school, building the schoolhouses to accommodate the vast hordes who have descended upon the educational system, and staffing the educational enterprise have been so serious that American educators may perhaps be forgiven their reluctance to face the question what the system is for and how it is to accomplish its purposes. Every time educators address themselves on the subject of education in America, they urge one another to redouble their efforts and forget their aims.

Our conception of the aims of education depends upon our philosophy in general. Philosophy is moribund throughout the world; and Americans are of all peoples the least inclined to philosophize. The most eminent philosophers who have lived in America in the last fifty years were Whitehead and Santayana, who were foreigners, and Dewey, whose philosophy is not, as I have suggested, a philosophy at all.

Besides, American educators have seen the obvious failures that have attended the attempts to build up educational theories. They can see that the doctrines of adaptation, immediate needs, and social reform lead nowhere. Does not this show the futility of trying to formulate a philosophy of education?

Then, too, if we succeeded in building a defensible theory of education, we should have to try to make our practice conform to it, and that might involve the re-education of educators, notoriously the most difficult of all educational tasks, and entrance upon the almost equally difficult program of interesting an entire population in things that ought to interest them, but now do not. If, for example, we decided that, since men are rational animals, they should develop their intellectual powers; and if we decided that all men should develop these powers, we should be required to help all men to acquire the intellectual techniques, such as reading, writing, and figuring, that the use of their intellectual powers demands, and compelled to interest them in ideas and in the intellectual tradition in which they live.

There is also in America a deep underlying conviction that the content of education is irrelevant. Higher education still carries with it a certain social standing, though this is becoming less and less significant as a larger and larger proportion of the population receives university degrees. As Gilbert and Sullivan remarked, when everybody is somebody, nobody is anybody. But, on the principle that what is honored in a country will be cultivated there, education is irrelevant because many of America's most venerated figures, like Edison, Rockefeller, and Ford, had little or none. The works of Horatio Alger, on which the boys of my generation were brought up, all depict an underprivileged lad, who through stalwart character, native shrewdness, and hard work becomes a millionaire. It is true that there is a rumor going around that education may be helpful in making you a millionaire, but, where this is believed, it is taken to mean vocational, not intellectual, education.

But meanwhile we do not know what to do with our children. If we can put them in school and have them stay there until we and the labor unions are ready to have them go to work, we can keep them out of harm's way, or at least out of worse places. The longer they are in school, the less we shall have to worry about them.

An imposing Commission of eminent educators and laymen appointed by President Truman recommended that the country look forward to doubling the number of students beyond the secondary schools by 1960. The basis for this proposal is the revelation, provided by the Army General Classification Test in the last war, that at least 49% of the college-age population has the ability to complete the first two years of college work and at least 32% has the ability to complete additional years of higher education. The Commission says, "These percentage figures supply conservative yet conclusive evidence of the social advisability of increased numbers attending college."

These percentage figures supply some evidence that a larger proportion of the college-age population has the ability to complete certain years of higher education as it is now carried on. They supply no evidence of the social advisability of having them do so. The argument that they should do so is based on the proposition that they have as much ability as those who are in college now. To know whether it is socially desirable to have them go to college, we should have to know whether it is socially desirable for all those who are in college now to be there, a question on which the Commission offers no evidence, and we should have to know why those who are not in college are not there. For example, it does not seem self-evident that a young man of twenty should be in higher education if he prefers to be somewhere else.

The Commission does not seem to care, still less to know, what these young people are to do in college when they get there. The education favored by the Commission is described in words so large and contradictory as to be meaningless. It wants an education "which is not only general and liberal, not only sufficiently vocational, not only for broad competence in citizenship and in the wise use of leisure, but also an integrated and meaningful combination of all these aims at successive levels of education in accordance with the potentialities of each." Such a summary I take to be a statement of the doctrine of no doctrine at all.

This impression is borne out by the more specific recommendations of the Commission, among which are that the colleges should train aviators, insurance salesmen, and photographers; and, if the community is a center for travelers from Latin America, the college should teach Spanish to the taxi-drivers. I am sure that the Commission would have recommended, if it had thought of it, that the college should also teach the taxi-drivers to drive taxis.

When the doctrine of no doctrine at all is in full swing, the educational program that emerges is determined by the tension between the interests of the teachers and those of the taught. Since we do not know what to teach our students, they might as well do what interests them. In many American institutions of higher learning that pride themselves on being progressive, it is now popular to say that there is no curriculum. The President's Commission on Higher Education has this to say of the dark, but unfortunately not distant, future: "As we bring more and more students to the campus, we shall increase in proportion the tremendous variety of human and social needs the college programs must meet. We shall add to the already overwhelming diversity of aptitudes, interests, and levels of attainment that characterize the student body. And so we shall have to increase the diversification of curricular offerings and of teaching methods and materials to correspond."

Since American institutions of higher education are already so diversified that they are split into a million fragments, the Commission's advice is a little like telling a drowning man that he can improve his position by drinking a great deal of water. Its program of infinite diversification rests on a *non sequitur*. Since men are different, the Commission holds that their education must be different. Since there is an infinite variety of individual differences, there must be an infinite variety of educational offerings.

There is no doubt that men are different. But they are also the same. One trouble with education in the West is that it has emphasized those respects in which men are different; this is what excessive specialization means. The purpose of basic education is to bring out our common humanity, a consummation more urgently needed today than at any time in the last five hundred years. To confuse at every point, as the Commission does, the education of our common humanity, which is primary and indispensable, with the education of our individual differences, which is secondary and in many cases unnecessary, is to get bad education at every point. What we have here is a prescription for the disintegration of society through the disintegration of the educational system. This process is now going on in the United States.

The limits imposed on this process are very wide. A university student in America may be able to elect almost any courses he chooses; he takes examinations in each of these courses given by the teacher who taught it. When he has taken the required number and passed with the minimum arithmetical average, he is pronounced an educated man. This means that the student will elect those courses which are the easiest, or which are offered at the most convenient times and places. I once knew a student who boasted that he had graduated from college without taking any course that was offered above the first floor.

Hence graduation from an American university is no guarantee of literacy. It is no guarantee that the American has any knowledge of the tradition in which, whether he knows it or not, he lives. This tradition is the Graeco-Hebraic tradition. I had a senior of the University of Chicago in one of my seminars who had never heard of Joshua, and six weeks ago I was interviewed in Paris by a prominent American journalist, a graduate of the University of Southern California, who had never heard of Thucydides or the Peloponnesian War.

Hence the failure of communication and community. When I was a student at Yale I could communicate only with those students who had happened, by accident, to elect the same courses that I had elected and whom I happened to know because I sat next to them in the lecture room. Since the seating arrangement was alphabetical, I could talk to Holden about Constitutional Law, to Hadden about German Literature, to Hosmer about Organic Evolution, and to Heffelfinger about Tennyson and Browning.

This system deprives the student of one of the greatest contributions that could be made to his education, the contribution of his fellow students. The disintegration of the course of study under the elective system, popularly called the "enrichment of the curriculum", has impoverished the colleges and universities of the United States by depriving them of any common intellectual life. Football and other extra-curriculum activities have achieved their exaggerated importance partly because the students have only these activities in common. So an undergraduate of a great American university wrote to the student newspaper not long ago and complained that the curriculum had now reached such richness that one student could not talk to another unless they both happened to remember the score of last Saturday's game.

The doctrine of adaptation, the doctrine of immediate needs, the doctrine of no doctrine at all, and the feeling that the content of education is irrelevant have a common basis. Americans are committed to the proposition that everybody must be educated. At the same time many American educators are convinced that everybody cannot be, in any definition of education that would have been accepted as recently as fifty years ago. At that time it was generally thought that education meant the development of the intellectual powers of men. Many

American educators believe that the intellectual powers of most men are so slight that it is not worthwhile to try to develop them. Still everybody must be educated. It is therefore necessary to bring forward a new definition of education, such as that it consists of adjusting the young to their environment or of meeting immediate needs. Or it is necessary to say that the content of education is irrelevant; that having everybody in school is the same thing as educating everybody.

Or to put it another way, the syllogism runs like this. Everybody has a right to education. But only a few are qualified for a good education. Those who are not qualified for a good education must be given a poor education, because everybody has a right to education. Anybody who favors a good education must, therefore, be anti-democratic, because only a few are qualified for a good education, and the true democrat insists on the education of all. The consequence is that those who believe in the capacity of the people are called reactionary and anti-democratic, whereas those who doubt the capacity of the people revel in the name of democrats and liberals.

In the report of the President's Commission on Higher Education, presented by men who have the deepest democratic convictions, we are urged in the name of democracy upon a course that divides the population into the mass and the élite. New institutions, continuing for two years beyond the secondary schools, will be established for the mass, who should not be allowed to clutter up existing institutions, because they are not bright enough. They should attend these colleges, because everybody should go to school as long as possible; but they should not be educated, in any recognizable sense of the word, because they are not capable of it. These new two-year colleges therefore become a kind of gigantic play-room in which the young are detained, or retarded, until we are ready to have them enter upon active life.

Because the conception of education as the development of the intellectual powers of men grew up at a time when society was aristocratic and education was limited to the few, the deeply convinced democrats who wrote the report of the President's Commission assume that anyone who favors an education designed to develop the intellectual powers of men must intend to limit it to the few. They most undemocratically assume that the mass of the people are incapable of achieving such an education. But they have no evidence for this, because the mass of the people have never had the chance to achieve it.

This paradoxical combination of strong faith in the political judgment of the masses with strong doubts of its intellectual capacities has a long history in America. Take the case of Thomas Jefferson. He was a celebrated democrat. He proposed that all children in Virginia should receive three years' free instruction in reading, writing, arithmetic, and geography. He said, "The mass of our citizens may be divided into two classes —the laboring and the learned . . . At the discharging of the pupils from the elementary schools, the two classes separate— those destined for labor will engage in the business of agriculture, or enter into apprenticeships to such handicraft art as may be their choice; their companions, destined to the pursuits of science, will proceed to the college . . ."

Three years of free education for all was doubtless a notable contribution to democratic practice in Jefferson's day. But the notion that it is possible to separate human beings at the age of nine or ten into those destined for labor and those destined for learning surpasses the fondest hopes of the psychological testers of our own time and seems to be an oligarchical notion. It seems to be based, not on the differences in the abilities of individuals, but on the differences in their social and economic background. Those destined for labor were destined for it primarily because they were the children of laboring men. Those destined for learning were destined for it because their fathers had wealth and leisure, and it was supposed that they would have them, too. These were the men who were to rule the commonwealth. They, and they alone, needed an intellectual education.

Yet the foundation of democracy is universal suffrage. It makes every man a ruler. If every man is a ruler, every man needs the education that rulers ought to have. If Jefferson did not see this, it may be because in his day the right to vote, and hence to rule, was still regarded as the privilege of the few who had inherited or acquired property. The kind of education we accept now when everybody is destined to rule is fundamentally an extension of the kind that in Jefferson's time was thought suitable to those destined to labor but not to rule. When we talk of our political goals, we admit the right of every man to be a ruler. When we talk of our educational program, we see no inconsistency in saying that only a few have the capacity to get the education that rulers ought to have. Yet the choice before us would seem to be clear: either we should abandon the democratic ideal or we should help every citizen to acquire the education that is appropriate to free men.

4: THE TRUE DOCTRINE[3]

The obvious failures of the doctrines of adaptation, immediate needs, social reform, and of the doctrine that we need no doctrine at all may suggest to us that we require a better definition of education. Let us concede that every society must have some system that attempts to adapt the young to their social and political environment. If the society is bad, in the sense, for example, in which the Nazi state was bad, the system will aim at the same bad ends. To the extent that it makes men bad in order that they may be tractable subjects of a bad state, the system may help to achieve the social ideals of the society. It may be what the society wants; it may even be what the society needs, if it is to perpetuate its form and accomplish its aims. In pragmatic terms, in terms of success in the society, it may be a "good" system.

But it seems to me clearer to say that, though it may be a system of training, or instruction, or adaptation, or meeting immediate needs, it is not a system of education. It seems clearer to say that the purpose of education is to improve men. Any system that tries to make them bad is not education, but something else. If, for example, democracy is the best form of society, a system that adapts the young to it will be an educational system. If despotism is a bad form of society, a system that adapts the young to it will not be an educational system, and the better it succeeds in adapting them the less educational it will be.

Every man has a function as a man. The function of a citizen or a subject may vary from society to society, and the system of training, or adaptation, or instruction, or meeting immediate needs may vary with it. But the function of a man as man is the same in every age and in every society, since it results from his nature as a man. The aim of an educational system is the same in every age and in every society where such a system can exist: it is to improve man as man.

If we are going to talk about improving men and societies, we have to believe that there is some difference between good and bad. This difference must not be, as the positivists think it is, merely conventional. We cannot tell this difference by any examination of the effectiveness of a given program as the pragmatists propose; the time required to estimate these effects is usually too long and the complexity of society is always too great for us to say that the consequences of a given program are altogether clear. We cannot discover the difference between good and bad by going to the laboratory, for men and societies are not laboratory animals. If we believe that there is no truth, there is no knowledge, and there are no values except those which are validated by laboratory experiment, we cannot talk about the improvement of men and societies, for we can have no standard of promoting or judging anything that takes place among men or in societies.

Society is to be improved, not by forcing a program of social reform down its throat, through the schools or otherwise, but by the improvement of the individuals who compose it. As Plato said, "Governments reflect human nature. States are not made out of stone or wood, but out of the characters of their citizens: these turn the scale and draw everything after them." The individual is the heart of society.

To talk about making men better we must have some idea of what men are, because if we have none, we can have no idea of what is good or bad for them. If men are brutes like other animals, there is no reason why they should not be trained as brutes are trained. A sound philosophy in general suggests that men are rational, moral, and spiritual beings and that the improvement of men means the fullest development of their rational, moral, and spiritual powers. All men have these powers, and all men should develop them to the fullest extent.

Man is by nature free, and he is by nature social. To use his freedom rightly he needs discipline. To live in society he needs the moral virtues. Good moral and intellectual habits are required for the fullest development of the nature of man.

To develop fully as a social, political animal man needs participation in his own government. A benevolent despotism will not do. You cannot expect the slave to show the virtues of the free man unless you first set him free. Only democracy, in which all men rule and are ruled in turn for the good life of the whole community, can be an absolutely good form of government.

The community rests on the social nature of men. Civilization is the deliberate pursuit of a common ideal. The good society is not just a society we happen to like or to be used to, as the positivists say. It is a community of good men.

Education deals with the development of the intellectual powers of men. Their moral and spiritual powers are the sphere of the family and the church. All three agencies must work in harmony; for, though a man has three aspects, he is still one man. But the schools cannot take over the role of the family and the church without promoting the atrophy of those institutions and failing in the task that is proper to the schools.

We cannot talk about the intellectual powers of men, though we can talk about training them, or amusing them, or adapting them, and meeting their immediate needs, unless our philosophy in general tells us that there is knowledge and that there is a difference between true and false. We must believe, too, that there are other means of obtaining knowledge than scientific experimentation. If valid knowledge can be sought only in the laboratory, many fields in which we thought we had knowledge will offer us nothing but opinion or superstition, and we shall be forced to conclude that we cannot know anything about the most important aspects of man and society. If we are to set about developing the intellectual powers of men through having them acquire knowledge of the most important subjects, we have to begin with the proposition that experimentation and empirical data will be of only limited use to us, contrary to the convictions of many American social scientists, and that philosophy, history, literature, and art give us knowledge, and significant knowledge, on the most significant issues.

If the object of education is the improvement of men, then any system of education that is without values is a contradiction in terms. A system that seeks bad values is bad. A system that denies the existence of values denies the possibility of education. Relativism, scientism, skepticism, and anti-intellectualism, the four horsemen of the philosophical apocalypse, have produced that chaos in education which will end in the disintegration of the West.

The prime object of education is to know what is good for man. It is to know the goods in their order. There is a hierarchy of values. The task of education is to help us understand it, establish it, and live by it. This Aristotle had in mind when he said: "It is not the possessions but the desires of men that must be equalized, and this is impossible unless they have a sufficient education according to the nature of things."

Such an education is far removed from the triviality of that produced by the doctrines of adaptation, of immediate needs, of social reform, or of the doctrine of no doctrine at all. Such an education will not adapt the young to a bad environment, but it will encourage them to make it good. It will not overlook immediate needs, but it will place these needs in their proper relationship to more distant, less tangible, and more important goods. It will be the only effective means of reforming society.

This is the education appropriate to free men. It is liberal education. If all men are to be free, all men must have this education. It makes no difference how they are to earn their living or what their special interests or aptitudes may be. They can learn to make a living, and they can develop their special interests and aptitudes, after they have laid the foundation of free and responsible manhood through liberal education. It will not do to say that they are incapable of such education. This claim is made by those who are too indolent or unconvinced to make the effort to give such education to the masses.

Nor will it do to say that there is not enough time to give everybody a liberal education before he becomes a specialist. In America, at least, the waste and frivolity of the educational system are so great that it would be possible through getting rid of them to give every citizen a liberal education and make him a qualified specialist, too, in less time than is now consumed in turning out uneducated specialists.

A liberal education aims to develop the powers of understanding and judgment. It is impossible that too many people can be educated in this sense, because there cannot be too many people with understanding and judgment. We hear a great deal today about the dangers that will come upon us through the frustration of educated people who have got educated in the expectation that education will get them a better job, and who then fail to get it. But surely this depends on the representations that are made to the young about what education is. If we allow them to believe that education will get them better jobs and encourage them to get educated with this end in view, they are entitled to a sense of frustration if, when they have got the education, they do not get the jobs. But, if we say that they should be educated in order to be men, and that everybody, whether he is a ditch-digger or a bank president, should have this education because he is a man, then the ditch-digger may still feel frustrated, but not because of his education.

Nor is it possible for a person to have too much liberal education, because it is impossible to have too much understanding and judgment. But it is possible to undertake too much in the name of liberal education in youth. The object of liberal education in youth is not to teach the young all they will ever need to know. It is to give them the habits, ideas, and techniques that they need to continue to educate themselves. Thus the object of formal institutional liberal education in youth is to prepare the young to educate themselves throughout their lives.

I would remind you of the impossibility of learning to understand and judge many of the most important things in youth. The judgment and understanding of practical affairs can amount to little in the absence of experience with practical affairs. Subjects that cannot be understood without experience should not be taught to those who are without experience. Or, if these subjects are taught to those who are without experience, it should be clear that these subjects can be taught only by way of introduction and that their value to the student depends on his continuing to study them as he acquires experience. The tragedy in America is that economics, ethics, politics, history, and literature are studied in youth, and never studied again. Therefore the graduates of American universities never understand them.

This pedagogical principle, that subjects requiring experience can be learned only by the experienced, leads to the conclusion that the most important branch of education is the education of adults. We sometimes seem to think of education as something like the mumps, measles, whooping-cough, or chicken-pox. If a person has had education in childhood, he need not, in fact he cannot, have it again. But the pedagogical principle that the most important things can be learned only in mature life is supported by a sound philosophy in general. Men are rational animals. They achieve their terrestrial felicity by the use of reason. And this means that they have to use it for their entire lives. To say that they should learn only in childhood would mean that they were human only in childhood.

And it would mean that they were unfit to be citizens of a republic.[4] A republic, a true *res publica,* can maintain justice, peace, freedom, and order only by the exercise of intelligence. When we speak of the consent of the governed, we mean, since men are not angels, who see the truth intuitively and do not have to learn it, that every act of assent on the part of the governed is a product of learning. A republic is really a common educational life in process. So Montesquieu said that, whereas the principle of a monarchy was honor, and the principle of a tyranny was fear, the principle of a republic was education.

Hence the ideal republic is the republic of learning. It is the utopia by which all actual political republics are measured. The goal toward which we started with the Athenians twenty-five centuries ago is an unlimited republic of learning and a world-wide political republic mutually supporting each other.

All men are capable of learning. Learning does not stop as long as a man lives, unless his learning power atrophies because he does not use it. Political freedom cannot endure unless it is accompanied by provision for the unlimited acquisition of knowledge. Truth is not long retained in human affairs without continual learning and relearning. Peace is unlikely unless there are continuous, unlimited opportunities for learning and unless men continuously avail themselves of them. The world of law and justice for which we yearn, the worldwide political republic, cannot be realized without the worldwide republic of learning. The civilization we seek will be achieved when all men are citizens of the world republic of law and justice and of the republic of learning all their lives long.

This continuous lifelong liberal education that makes a man a citizen of the world republic of learning and that is indispensable if he is to do his part to bring about the world republic of law and justice is an intellectual discipline that fits a man to solve new problems as they arise, to grasp new facts as they appear, to meet new needs as they present themselves, and to remould the environment to make it conform to the aspirations of the human spirit.

The pedagogical content of this education may be simply stated. The liberally educated man must know how to read, write, and figure. He must know and understand the ideas that have animated mankind. He must comprehend the tradition in which he lives. He must be able to communicate with his fellow-men. Through familiarity with the best models he must have constantly before him that habitual vision of greatness without which, Whitehead said, any true education is impossible.

The process of such an education should be dialectical. The liberally educated man should be able to continue the Great Conversation that began in the dawn of history, that goes on at the present day, and that is best exemplified by the Socratic dialogue.

Socrates collected opinions, asked questions, clarified terms and ideas, and indicated commitments. That is all he did. All that was required of those who took part with him was that they should try to think and to understand one another. They did not have to agree with Socrates, before or after. They did not have to agree among themselves. If they came to conviction, they did so by their own free will. The only constraint upon them was the law of contradiction. They could not answer Yes and No to the same question at the same time.

As a sound philosophy in general teaches us that men are rational beings, so the educational philosophy dependent on it tells us that though men can be assisted to learn, they can learn only by themselves. They cannot be indoctrinated without violation of the laws of their nature. Criticism, discussion, question, debate—these, are the truly human methods of instruction. Teaching, like midwifery, is a co-operative art. The great truth that Plato presented, somewhat romantically, in the dialogue called the *Meno,* as the doctrine of reminiscence, is that intellectual progress does not take place when the teacher is laying down the law and the pupil is memorizing it, but when teacher and pupil are working together to bring the pupil to the rational answer to the question before him. The Socratic dialogue is the great mirror of pedagogy, whether the student is a child or an adult.

The Socratic dialogue, too, may provide us with a model for the university, the institution that stands at the apex of the educational system and that eventually determines the character of all the rest of it.

In a paper written for the tercentenary of Harvard, Alfred North Whitehead said that the task of the universities is intellectual leadership and proposed that Harvard should fashion the mind of the twentieth century as the University of Paris fashioned that of the Middle Ages.

When I read Mr. Whitehead's article, I asked myself whether the universities had ever exerted intellectual leadership or had ever fashioned the mind of any epoch except the Middle Ages. Since the universities were not established till the Middle Ages, they could not have fashioned the mind of the ages before. As to the ages afterward, their minds were fashioned by individual men, or by small groups of men, most of whom were not associated with universities. One of the most striking things about the works that have made the minds of various ages is that almost none of them were written by professors. And where they were written by men who were sheltered by universities, the men and not the universities were responsible. That Newton worked at Cambridge should not blind us to the fact that in his day the British universities were sinking into a deep torpor, probably brought on by port, from which they were not to awaken for more than a hundred and fifty years. The influences that have been most effective on a world scale in fashioning the mind of the twentieth century up to now are Marx, Darwin, and Freud, not Heidelberg, Oxford, or the Sorbonne.

Ever since Mr. Whitehead's article appeared I have been trying to figure out how it was that the universities fashioned the mind of the Middle Ages when they have not been able to do so since. In order to discover whether the universities can exert intellectual leadership again, we have to find out how they did so once. Mr. Whitehead's answer was *suggestiveness*. They did it by suggestiveness, and suggestiveness comes from action. So Mr. Whitehead said that the way Harvard could do for modern times what the University of Paris did for the Middle Ages was to absorb into itself those schools of vocational training for which systematized understanding has importance.

This answer seemed inadequate to me thirteen years ago and has grown more so with every passing day. If this is all there is to it, the American universities should long since have fashioned the mind of this age, for they have absorbed into themselves not only all those vocational schools for which systematized understanding has importance, but also every other vocational school, so that the ordinary American university presents an array of vocational schools of incredible variety and insignificance.

What is important for us is not the fact that the medieval universities entered into the life of their time, but the way in which they did it. In the Middle Ages the whole university was both speculative and practical. The insight that produced this organization was that everything speculative has significance in the practical dimension, and everything practical, to be worth study, must have a speculative basis. The purpose for which any action was studied or taught was to increase the understanding of that action and what it implied. Not every occupation was a profession in the Middle Ages. A profession was a body of men trained in a subject matter that had intellectual content in its own right. The aim of the group was the common good. The universities of the Middle Ages did not enter into the life of their time through having schools that actually or ostensibly prepared men for vocations, but through a combination of the speculative and the practical that made the two indistinguishable as subjects of study and teaching.

The disciplines of the Middle Ages were studied together because they were lived together, and must be. Professors and students had a common heritage in the tradition of learning. They had a common training in the methods and techniques appropriate to each discipline. They did not necessarily agree on what ideas were basic, but they did have a common acquaintance with the ideas that could seriously claim to be basic and a commensurate ability, derived from a common training, to appraise and understand those ideas. The characteristic intellectual apparatus of the medieval university, as Mill nostalgically points out in his essay *On Liberty*, was the disputation, which has now disappeared from the Anglo-Saxon world.

If it is these features of the medieval university, rather than its specifically vocational interests, that helped the University of Paris to fashion the mind of the Middle Ages, we can understand why no universities since the Middle Ages have been able to duplicate the accomplishments of those which existed then.

In the essay that he wrote for the Harvard tercentenary, Etienne Gilson pointed out that the scholars of the Middle Ages wanted to universalize the faith. They had a strong belief in the universal character of rational truth. "Since faith could not possibly be proved by reason," Mr. Gilson says, "the only hope of universalizing it was to make it acceptable to reason." The method of seeking to make faith acceptable to reason was endless argumentation. Mr. Gilson concludes: "Thus did it come to pass that, viewing themselves as members of the same spiritual family, using a common language to impart to others the same fundamental truth, those medieval scholars succeeded in living and working together for about three centuries, and so long as they did, there was in the world, together with a vivid feeling for the universal character of truth, some sort of Occidental unity."

The end of the Middle Ages brought with it great gains in every field of knowledge, except possibly philosophy and theology. The medieval period had been an age of debate. What followed was age upon age of discovery. Inquiry was promoted by specialization and the experimental method. In the Middle Ages the members of the University of Paris thought together. The subjects that were studied were studied together. Teachers and students tried to see everything in relation to everything else. They had to—their object was understanding through discussion. The discoverer or the experimenter, on the other hand, had to be a specialist as soon as possible; his demands gradually broke down the common training of the medieval period. Since his object was to open new fields, he did not care for the tradition of learning. Descartes, for example, began by repudiating all previous thinkers.

As the specialties multiplied, specialists could not think together. The specialties were too numerous and diverse to be studied together. The discussion that was the principal activity of the medieval university had to stop. The standard by which the medieval university determined what should be studied had to go. Anything that any specialist wanted to study had to be included. Who could say that one vocational school was any more appropriate to a university than any other?

The processes of the last eight hundred years have been favorable to the formal emancipation and education of the people. But in a period of discovery, a period of specialization and esoteric experiment, what can their education be? Almost by definition nobody can know anything except a specialist, and he can know nothing outside his specialty. At the same time all the wonderful things that are happening in science can be made exciting to the people, and a profit is to be garnered by writing them up in a cheerful and inaccurate way for popular consumption.

So Hermann Hesse, in his novel *Magister Ludi,* calls this the "Age of the Digest." This is the period of the fragmentary, the topical, the diverting—the period of the uncomprehended trifle. It is a period of propaganda and publicity.

The most remarkable paradox of our time is that, in proportion as the instruments of communication have increased in number and power, communication has steadily declined. Mutual intelligibility is probably a rarer phenomenon now than at any time in history.

The task of intellectual leadership now is to bring about a genuine communion of minds. But this is still the age of discovery. It is, therefore, still the age of the individual thinker, of the specialist. And, as a consequence, it is the age of the digest, with all the incoherence and triviality that must characterize such an age. If there is to be a new cultural epoch and not simply a further cultural collapse, the distinguishing feature of the new epoch must be this: it must combine discovery and discussion. The object must be, while retaining and encouraging the drive toward discovery, to restore the conditions of conversation.

If then we ask how the university can repeat the brilliant leadership of the University of Paris, and if the task of that leadership is to bring about a genuine communion of minds through the restoration of the conditions of conversation, we run at once against the fact that in the speculative realm the modern university is chaotic, that in the practical realm it is silent, and that the two realms are sharply divided from each other. The chaos in the speculative realm means that ideas are unclear, unrelated, and uncomprehended. The silence in the practical realm means that on matters of life or death to our society no disinterested voice reaches the public. The division of the speculative and the practical impoverishes both. The conditions of conversation do not exist within the university. In the academic world there is no genuine communion of minds.

One of the things most often proposed as a step toward communion of minds is international co-operation in science, art, and scholarship. Although such co-operation should be promoted, it would not do much to establish a community within a university, or within a country, or throughout the world. A scholar in one country can now communicate with another scholar in the same field anywhere in the West. He is usually incapable of communicating with a scholar in another field on his own campus. If the university as such, the university as distinguished from its individual members, is to exert intellectual leadership toward creating a genuine communion of minds, it must first have such communion within itself.

The task of bringing about communion within a modern university can be performed, if it can be performed at all, only through a common training, a common appreciation of the different kinds of knowledge and of the different methods and techniques appropriate to each, and a common, continuous discussion on the Socratic model of those ideas which can pretend to be important, together with the consideration of the practical implications of those ideas.

In such a community, men, even if they disagree, should be able to relate what they are thinking to what others are thinking or have thought on the same point and on all points connected with it. The individual should be able to locate himself in a universe of discourse. Ideally, enough unity should prevail in the world of thought so that no idea, no theory, doctrine, or general view of things could exist in isolation from the rest.

A university should be an intellectual community in which specialists, discoverers, and experimenters, in addition to their obligation to their specialties, recognize an obligation to talk with and understand one another. If they can restore the conditions of conversation among themselves, they can become a university, a corporate body of thinkers, that can exert intellectual leadership and hope to make some modest efforts to fashion the mind of its time. They could hope to achieve a *Summa Dialectica,* a summation of the possibilities of thought, of the methods of analyzing, relating, and understanding ideas, with an indication of real agreements and disagreements. It may not be possible to reconcile the ideologies that now divide the world. But we cannot tell whether or not they can be reconciled until we have first tried to get them clear.

The problem, then, is to retain the values of the age of

discovery, to regain those of the age of debate, and to put an end to the age of the digest. And the problem is to do this through the university as a whole, not through individuals who happen to reside in it. To do this it would have to think as a university, and think both speculatively and practically. The intelligence of the university as such would have to be focused on great speculative and practical issues.

If, then, some modern sage, like Mr. Whitehead, were to ask once more how a university might exert intellectual leadership and fashion the mind of the twentieth century, he might create for himself a sort of myth or dream of the higher learning. In this myth he might fancy that the university, in addition to making the most sensational discoveries in all fields of knowledge, asked itself what were the crucial problems of contemporary civilization upon which the intelligence of the university might shed some light. He might see the university studying such questions as the crisis in our culture, the conflict between East and West, the relations of church and state, or the responsibility of the public for the health of the community, and giving its impartial advice to a people distracted by propaganda. He might imagine that even the specialized, theoretical thought of the university would be enriched and a genuine communion of minds advanced by this effort to focus the intellect of the university upon the continuing problems of human society.

Of course the sage would be enough of a sage to realize that the ideas that were brought to bear upon practical problems could not originate in or be validated by any official creed, dogma, or authority. In his dream the university would be aiming at restoring the conditions of conversation and reinterpreting basic ideas. Thus he would see the university taking up one such idea after another and discussing, clarifying, and modifying it in the light of modern discoveries. This would be the creation of a *Summa Dialectica*. He would see the university as a whole, the university as such, moving in both the speculative and the practical orders toward communion, unity, understanding, and the enlightenment of the world.

This is, of course, merely a myth, or a dream. And I fear that it will always remain so. I fear that the university, in

Europe as well as in America, is so far sunk in empiricism, specialism, and positivism that we cannot look to it to repeat in our time the brilliant leadership of the University of Paris. What, then, is the world to do for intellectual leadership, which it needs more today than at any time in the past five hundred years?

I suggest that we may require another institution, which would leave the university to go on as it is doing now, which would not supplant the university, but which would take up the burden the university has laid down.

Such an institution would be composed of men who were prepared to conduct a continuous Socratic dialogue on the basic issues of human life. They would be specialists, but they would have passed beyond specialism. They would bring their specialized training and points of view to bear upon the common task of clarification and understanding. They would be prepared to think, both speculatively and practically; they would be able to communicate with one another and with the public. They would retain the advantages of the Age of Discovery and regain those of the Age of Debate.

They would establish a genuine communion of minds. They would know no limitations of national boundaries; for they could be assembled from all parts of the world. They could therefore at once advance and symbolize that world community, that world republic of learning, without which the world republic of law and justice is impossible.

They might give light to the nations now wandering in darkness. They might fashion the mind of the 20th century and make it equal to the dreadful obligations that Providence has laid upon it.

The Gottesman Lectures, Uppsala University, 1951

FOUR

EDUCATION AND INDEPENDENT THOUGHT

The best definition of a university that I have been able to think of is that it is a center of independent thought. Such centers are indispensable to the progress, and even to the security, of any society. Perhaps the short lives that dictatorships have enjoyed in the past are attributable as much to this as to any other single thing: dictatorship and independent thought cannot exist together; and no society can flourish long without independent thought.

Independent thought implies criticism, and criticism is seldom popular in time of war or danger of war. At such times every effort is made to compel conformity of opinion of the entire population, and the country often goes into an ecstasy of tribal self-adoration. This loss of balance is unfortunate for the country. The United States suffered more from the elimination of Germanic studies during the first World War than Germany did, and we have had to do a quick about-face in our attitude toward Japan and Germany since the second War. If war is for the sake of peace—and no one will contend that it is an end in itself—then we have to think, when war is imminent, where we shall be and what we shall do when it is over. Such thinking is difficult to do amidst cries of "unconditional surrender" addressed to the enemy and "traitor" addressed to those citizens who disagree with the majority opinion of the moment.

Independent thought is valuable, even in a crisis. Perhaps it is especially valuable then. But to appreciate its value, even in such "normal" times as we enjoyed before 1917, requires a degree of understanding of education, universities, and intellectual activity in general that the American people do not yet seem to have attained. I do not underestimate the tremendous contribution America has made in originating and applying the doctrine of education for all, nor the generosity with which her citizens have supported her educational institutions. When education is defined, however, as a means to a better job or a higher social position and intellectual activity is appraised in terms of its immediate material benefits, popular support of education does not compel revision of my suspicion that the American people do not yet set a proper value on independent thought. We have a great tendency to substitute names for things. The American people are devoted to the name of education. If they can find something that they can call education, but that is really something else, like schooling or training or housing or exercising the young, they will enthusiastically support it, and at the same time they will be indifferent to, and even fearful of, true education. True education is the improvement of men through helping them learn to think for themselves.

Since a university faculty is a group set apart to think independently and to help other people to learn to do so, it is fatal to force conformity upon it. Nobody would argue that all professors must be members of the Republican Party; but we seem to be approaching the point where they will all be required to be either Republicans or Democrats. I do not claim that the status of university professor should entitle a man to exemption from the laws. But I do say that imposing regulations that go beyond the laws is impractical and dangerous. There are fashions in opinion as well as in behavior. We have just emerged from an era in which a schoolteacher could lose her job by smoking, dancing, or using cosmetics. We should avoid entering one in which a professor can lose his post and his reputation by holding views of politics, economics, or international relations that are not acceptable to the majority. This is thought control.

The suggestion that professors should take special oaths or make special statements of their loyalty causes resentment in university faculties because of the dangers to which I have referred in going beyond the laws. If there are spies or traitors on the faculties of universities, they can be dealt with under laws already on the books. Such persons, if there are any, will gladly take oaths and sign statements attesting their loyalty.

Perhaps the most important reason for the resentment of university faculties at the proposal that they should be given special tests for loyalty is their fear that it portends an effort on the part of the government, or of the public or its representatives, to assume control over the course of study, the program of research, and the qualifications of the members of the faculty. In view of what is going on in many parts of the country, this fear is not unjustified. Since academic bodies have from time immemorial asserted their right to the sole determination of these matters, since this is their most sacred and essential prerogative, and since the transfer of this prerogative to any external agency might lead to the disintegration of the university and the collapse of its standards, the objections of faculties to anything looking in this direction are comprehensible and correct.

I do not attach much importance to the argument sometimes advanced by professors that in an age of specialization only a professor of engineering can appraise an educational program, or a research project, or another professor, in engineering. Anybody who has had any experience in academic administration knows that there is such a thing as departmental self-adoration and that it is not confined to the good departments. The votes of faculties sometimes seem to reflect the competition of vested interests rather than a considered judgment on educational policy. It is true that the extreme specialization of our day makes it hard for one outside the field to form an intelligent estimate of the work and the workers within it. It is equally true that specialization has divorced the specialist from the understanding of fields outside his own and hence from a comprehension of the problems and policies of other departments and of the university as a whole. Nevertheless, if we have to choose between the myopic egocentricity of internal control and the blind bumbling of external control, I should prefer the former.

External control by definition prevents universities from being centers of independent thought. By definition, if they are dominated by outside agencies or influences, they are not independent and can engage in independent thought only by sufferance. Such sufferance is likely to be short-lived in the absence of a clear understanding and a strong tradition supporting independent thought. As I have said, there are few traces of this understanding and this tradition in the United States. It does not make very much difference where the legal control of a university lies if the tradition governing its exercise requires that the wishes of the faculty in regard to curriculum, research, and staff must be respected.

A commission in Great Britain and one in the United States have recently studied the press and come to the same conclusion, that what is needed is not control, but criticism. The freedom of the press is too important to be lost; the irresponsibility of the press is too dangerous to be ignored. Unlike the press, the universities are subjected to a good deal of criticism, most of it from the press, and much of it haphazard and uninformed. I do not know of any irresponsible universities, though the Oxford described by Gibbon and Adam Smith shows that such a thing is not impossible. In our day the gross error of the universities is not that they luxuriate in slothful self-admiration but that they are too responsive to public whims. Behind every deplorable aspect of university life, and there are a good many of them, is some public pressure. An extreme example is the criticism that was visited in the columns of a newspaper of large circulation upon the University of Notre Dame for wasting its money in expanding its educational plant when it should be enlarging its stadium. This may suggest to us that there is a difference between being responsible and being responsive.

In order to guarantee the independence of members of the faculties most universities give them permanent tenure when they reach a certain rank. This is in recognition of the fact that their purpose in life cannot be achieved if their thinking is subject to the control of presidents, chancellors, trustees, regents, or the public. Of course mistakes cannot be avoided in the appointment of professors to permanent tenure. Some men may incorrectly be suspected of the ability to think; others may stop thinking when they have arrived at life tenure. This is the price that is paid for the independence of professors, which is another way of saying that it is part of the price that is paid for the greatness of a university.

Tenure is valuable, for, like an insurance policy, it is a provision for unpleasant contingencies. Like an insurance policy, it cannot provide for all contingencies, and, in the worst, it is quickly swept away. Runaway inflation or general bankruptcy will wipe out the protection of insurance; mass hysteria will do the same to tenure. The record shows that the professors at the University of California were entitled to think that they had tenure; it was a great talking point, but at the last it turned out to be nothing but a talking point. The professors lost their positions. And everywhere in the United States, university professors, whether or not they have tenure, are silenced by the general atmosphere of repression that now prevails. The legal protection of tenure should be retained; but its limitations should be recognized; and it should be recognized, too, that those limitations cannot be overcome by any legal devices, but only be informing and arousing public opinion.

In addition to being a member of a university faculty a professor is a citizen. When a man becomes a professor, he does not become a second-class citizen, disabled from saying, doing, or joining anything that other citizens may legally say, do, or join. The university assumes no control over his activities as a citizen and takes no responsibility for them. Since the professor is always referred to by his title, the university is brought into his activities as a citizen, and its public relations may suffer as a result. Of course, they may also benefit. Whether they suffer or benefit will depend in part on the temper of the times. The public relations of Columbia and Johns Hopkins doubtless benefited when Professor Jessup and Professor Lattimore began to serve the country. They doubtless suffered when Senator McCarthy presented his charges against them. I think it will not be argued that a professor should decline to take a public post or to express himself on a controversial question for fear that Senator McCarthy or someone like him may call him a Communist.

What then are the limitations on the freedom of the faculty? They are the limitations on independent thought. These should be nothing more than the laws of logic and the laws of the country. I would hope that the laws of the country would not seek to control thought. I do not believe that any legislative body can repeal or amend the law of contradiction. I do not see how it is possible to say that the same thing is both true and not true at the same time in the same respect, and I should think it difficult to conduct any communication within the community of scholars unless they all accept the law of contradiction. I should not suggest any other limitations, and if any professor wanted to show, as some of my colleagues do, that the law of contradiction has been repealed by modern scientific advances, I should encourage him to pursue his outrageous course. If a professor can think and make his contribution to a center of independent thought, that is all that is required of him. One might wish that he were more agreeable or more conventional; but he cannot be discharged because he fails to measure up to desirable standards in these respects. As long as his political activities are legal, he may engage in them.

As to Communism, we see first that it is a subject that is worth thinking about and should be studied in universities. Almost everybody agrees to this. The opposite point of view is sufficiently dealt with by the story of the university president who met an alumnus who said, "Well, Mr. President, still teaching Communism in the College?" The President replied: "Yes, still teaching Communism in the College and cancer in the medical school."

Must we say that Communism can be taught only by those who are opposed to it, as the professors in the medical school are opposed to cancer? We would not appoint a professor in medicine who was earnestly trying to see to it that every member of the community got cancer. Can we permit the appointment of a man who is trying to make us all Communists? If he is a spy or advocating the overthrow of the government by violence, we cannot. But convinced and able Marxists on the faculty may be necessary if the conversation about Marxism is to be anything but hysterical and superficial. It may be said that a Marxist cannot think and that therefore he is not eligible for membership in a university community according to my definition of it. I admit that the presumption is to this effect; but I must add that regarding the presumption as irrefutable comes dangerously close to saying that anybody who does not agree with me cannot think.

I do not know a great deal about the inner working of the Communist Party in America. It is represented as a conspiracy, with everybody in it under iron discipline, which I take to mean that its members and supporters have given up the privilege of independent thought and have surrendered themselves entirely to the Party. If this is so, a member of the Communist Party cannot qualify as a member of the university community in any field that is touched by Party policy, tradition, or discipline. The Party has apparently taken a strong line in biology, music, and literature; and I suppose that at any time it could lay down what should be believed in astronomy and archaeology, if it has not done so already. If a man is not free to think independently, he is no use to a center of independent thought. The presumption is strong that there are few fields in which a member of the Communist Party can think independently.

But what if we should find a member of the Communist Party who, in spite of this presumption, did think independently? The fact of membership cannot and should not disqualify him from membership in the faculty of a university in view of the additional fact that he does not act as members of the Party are supposed to act. I cannot insist too strongly that the primary question in every case is what is this individual man himself, not what are the beliefs and activities of his relatives, associates, and acquaintances. When the life of the individual has been exposed before us for many years, and when he has neither acted nor taught subversively, the doctrine of guilt by association can have slight value. A man who is a bad member of the Communist Party may conceivably be qualified to be a professor, because he has retained his independence; and a good member of the Party may be qualified to be a professor if he retains his independence in the field in which he teaches and conducts his research.

I use these examples to make my position clear and not because they ever occurred in my experience. Whether I would have had the courage to recommend to our Board the appointment of a Marxist, or a bad member of the Communist Party, or a good member whose field was not affected by the Party line is very dubious indeed. But in the most unlikely event that such persons ever came over my academic horizon, uniquely qualified to conduct teaching and research in their chosen fields, I ought to have had the courage to say that they should be appointed without regard to their political views or associations. The reason why I ought to is that it is of the first importance to insist that the popularity or unpopularity of a man's political views and associations shall not determine whether or not he may be a professor. If we once let go of the Constitution and the laws as marking out the area in which a professor is free to operate as a citizen and of the ability to think independently as establishing the standard he must meet as a scholar, we are lost.

What I have said of course applies with greater force to those members of university faculties who have joined so-called Communist front organizations. I have never, so far as I know, joined one of these, but the fact that I have to say "so far as I know" suggests the dangers now involved in joining anything. When a man is asked by a person he trusts to join an organization for stated purposes which he shares, it seems pusillanimous not to accept. Hardly a day passes that I do not feel pusillanimous, because I must now refuse to associate myself with anything without knowing the political views of every other person who is associated or who may later become associated with the movement. This is, of course, the most lamentable aspect of the present situation. It is the creeping miasma of intimidation. If one believes, as I do, that the progress of mankind depends upon the freest possible expression of diverse points of view, one must feel that we have come to a sort of halting place in American history. The American people, with a revolutionary tradition, a tradition of independence and toleration, now find themselves blocking the revolutionary aspirations of oppressed peoples abroad and declining at home to permit the kind of criticism that has been our glory, and I think our salvation, in the past.

How do we determine whether a professor can think? The competence of a professor in his chosen field should be determined by those who are qualified to have an opinion. If a professor is held to be incompetent by those admittedly expert in the field, he cannot complain that it is unjust to relieve him of his post. The activities of a professor as a citizen, however unpopular they may make him or the university, can be called in question, like those of other citizens, only by the duly constituted public authorities, and they can act only under the law. Education and research require the best men. They will not enter academic life if it carries special disabilities with it.

Even when a professor's peers believe that he is incompetent and recommend his dismissal great care must be taken to see to it that he is not a victim of the prejudices of his colleagues. Professors do not like unconventional people any better than the rest of the population does. A professor has, or is likely to have, a vested interest in his subject, or even in his point of view about his subject. The man who is breaking new ground, and who consequently thinks that most of his colleagues are wrong in their points of view, will hardly be the most popular member of the faculty. Geniuses have had a hard time as professors in America. Every effort must be made to protect the originality as well as the independence of the thinking in a university.

Like most other chancellors and presidents I spent a considerable part of my life defending professors with whom I did not agree. A principle is no good unless it is good in a crisis and unless it applies to those who hold views opposite to yours as well as to those who share your opinions. It makes no difference, therefore, whether or not the chief executive of a university likes and agrees with a professor; he must defend his independence because the life of the university is at stake.

Professors are not employees, either of the chief executive or of the board of trustees. They are members of an academic community. The aim of the community is independent thought. This requires the defense of the independence of its members.

I know, too, that by my standard no perfect university exists in the United States. This is merely saying that, human institutions being what they are, they must always fall short of the ideal. What I am seeking is the definition of the ideal, which is the criterion by which universities must be measured. If we know where we ought to be going, we can tell whether we are on the right path. The perfect university cannot arise unless we know what a perfect one would be. The indispensable condition to the rise of the perfect university is the guarantee of the independence of the university and its members. The infringement of the independence of the universities and professors that we have today means that we can never get the kind of universities and professors we should have.

I do not claim that professors are the only people who can think or the only people who do. I merely say that unless a man can and will think he should not be a professor, and that professors are the only people in the world whose sole duty is to think. To require them to stop thinking, or to think like everybody else, is to defeat the purpose of their lives and of their institution.

I recognize, too, that these are dangerous times and that the state must take precautions against those who would subvert it. I do not suggest that those who want to force conformity upon academic bodies do so from any but the most patriotic motives. I do say that they are misguided. The methods they have chosen cannot achieve the result they seek. They will, on the contrary, imperil the liberties we are fighting for, the most important of which are freedom of thought, speech, and association. If we cannot ourselves understand and apply our own principles, we cannot expect the rest of the world to rally to them. Since the struggle in which we are engaged is one for the loyalty and adherence of mankind, the clarity and conviction with which we hold our own principles are at least as important as our military strength. The question of freedom of thought, speech, and association is much more than an academic question.

How can we reconcile this conception of a university with the facts of its legal control? The legal control, we find, is not so important as the manner and degree of its exercise. Oxford and Cambridge are in effect operated by their own faculties, though subject to occasional governmental investigation and criticism. The European universities are operated by the governments, though the governments are restricted by public opinion to a kind of management that preserves the ancient rights of the faculties. Both kinds of control require a high degree of responsibility on the part of those who have legal or quasi-legal control.

The American universities are organized on the model of the big business corporation, which leads to all kinds of temptations to analogize them in every respect to such corporations. But there are important differences. The American endowed university is like the United States Steel Corporation in that it has a board of directors and a management; but it is different in that there are no stockholders, there is no profit-and-loss statement, and there are, on the academic side, no employees. The responsibility of the board of trustees, as long as it stays within the law, is to its own conscience. The measure of the prosperity of the institution cannot be found in any report of its financial condition. The quality of the university is determined by the quality of its faculty, whom the board of trustees cannot select and whose work they cannot direct.

Obviously a high degree of responsibility, forbearance, and understanding are required of trustees under the American system if they are to allow it to become a center of independent thought and are not to follow the natural lines suggested by the fact that a large university looks like any other large corporation. The complete legal control of the board of regents or trustees is undoubted. But as the Minister of Education in a European country is required to restrain the impulse to use his legal powers because of the traditional rights of faculties, and the faculties of Oxford and Cambridge are not irresponsible, though they might be if they wished, so the American board of trustees, in spite of its legal control of the university, should limit itself to criticism of the educational and scientific program of the university, to the conservation and development of its funds, and to the interpretation of the university to the public. Those who have the legal control should be wise enough to refrain from exercising it. In this view the trustees become not the managers of the university, but its best friends and severest critics, laymen who are interested in the university, who believe in it, and who wish to assist it. I do not subscribe to the notion that the board should operate the university as the representative of the community. Nor do I subscribe to the notion that the board is a kind of supreme court that should decide educational issues brought before it. This would mean that the Board would be determining the educational policy of the institution, something that even the best boards are not qualified to do.

An extreme statement of this position would be that the faculties could ask the trustees or regents to take an oath supporting the aims of the faculties, since the principal duty of trustees and regents is to further those aims, but that the trustees and regents could not exact such expressions from faculties in regard to the aims of trustees and regents. To put the extreme position another way: a trustee, or a board of trustees, who did not like what the faculty or a faculty member was doing should resign. It should never occur to trustees that faculty members should resign because they do not share the opinions of trustees. The most important right that the trustees have is the right of criticism. I think that two propositions are true: first, a university is a center of independent thought, and second, uncriticized groups inevitably deteriorate. The solution of the problem lies, then, not in regulation or in control, but in criticism.

The difficulty is money. Universities always need money. Even those which have the most can always see ways in which they could use more. How can they get more except by being responsive to public whims? How can they get it if they are independent? The tax-supported universities must get their money from legislatures. The endowed universities must get theirs from contributors, and the contributors who could do the most are those with the most money. The present primacy of public relations in the management of universities, the view that they must ingratiate themselves with the public, and in particular with the most wealthy and influential portions of it, the doctrine that a university may properly frame its policies in order to get money and that it may properly teach or study whatever it can get financed—these notions are ruinous to a university in any rational conception of it. They are on a par with what is perhaps the most widely held and most erroneous notion about university management, that the principal duty of the chief executive is to raise money. The principal duty of the chief executive of a university is to produce a university that deserves support. His secondary duty is to raise the money to support it.

So public relations are secondary. The policy of the university should not be formulated with a view to its public relations. Its public relations should be formulated with a view to its policies. A university should not adopt a policy because it will bring money. It should work out its program and then get it financed. In the long run difficulties encountered in financing a good program will be less embarrassing than success in financing a bad one.

Most of the discussion of higher education in the United States is about money. Money is very important; but we ought to think once in a while about the things that money cannot do. The only problems that money can solve are financial problems. Money cannot make a great university; it can only supply the means to one. We know that millions are spent annually on enterprises called educational that have no educational value. Money cannot even buy men, because the best men will not stay long in an institution that has nothing but money. If an institution has an idea, it can use money to realize it. If it has no ideas, all the money in the world will not help it. The important problems of American education are intellectual, not financial. In this situation there is grave danger in money, for there are numerous instances in which money has been spent for purposes that could not be achieved or that should not be achieved, with the result that the institution where it was spent and the educational system as a whole have been deformed.

We all know that beautiful buildings and expensive equipment do not make a great university. Some of the best work at the University of Chicago came out of the poorest quarters. Which would be better, a faculty of a thousand, average fair; or a faculty of five hundred, average excellent? A large and mediocre faculty will cost more than a small but superior one. Its effect is diffuse; its example is uninspiring, and consequently it is difficult to rally the public to its support or its defense.

With transportation what it is today I do not see why every university should try to teach and study everything. Some subjects do not seem to me to have reached the teaching stage, yet we are ardently engaged in teaching them. Other subjects have not the staff available for instruction everywhere. Others can be adequately dealt with if they are studied in a few places. The present passion for cyclotrons seems to me excessive. The infinite proliferation of courses is repulsive. There is a good deal of evidence, I think, that the educational system as a whole needs less money rather than more. The reduction in its income would force it to reconsider its expenditures. The expectation that steadily increasing funds will be forthcoming justifies the maintenance of activities that ought to be abandoned; it justifies waste.

Some waste is inevitable; but the amount that we find in some universities is disgraceful. These institutions carry on extravagant enterprises that by no stretch of the imagination can be called educational, and then plead poverty as the reason for their financial campaigns. The self-interest of professors, the vanity of administrators, trustees, and alumni, and the desire to attract public attention are more or less involved in these extravagances. Yet the result of them is that the institution is unintelligible and, in every sense of the word, insupportable.

The California loyalty oath originated in the desire of the administration to get money from the legislature. As this genesis suggests, the chief danger to American education is that it will sell its birthright for a mess of pottage. The danger to it is that in seeking money it will sacrifice the purposes for which it exists. I have enough faith in the intelligence and generosity of the American people to believe that they will understand and support universities that have principles, that will try to make them clear, and that will stick to them. Every time a university takes another step in the direction of the service-station conception, or the public-entertainment conception, or the housing-project conception of the higher learning, every time it makes a concession to public pressure in order to get money, every time it departs from the idea of a university as a center of independent thought, it increases the confusion in the public mind about what a university is and makes it more difficult to present any rational appeal for the independence that true universities are entitled to. The universities are themselves largely responsible for the lack of understanding of education and of universities and of intellectual activity of which I have complained.

The university should be the symbol of the highest powers and aspirations of mankind. Mankind aspires to achieve human felicity through the exercise of reason. Independent thought is the ultimate reliance of the race. Abandoning vanity and sham, the universities should dedicate themselves to their great symbolic task. Upon their performance of this task rests their claim to freedom.

February 20, 1952

FIVE

THE ADMINISTRATOR: LEADER OR OFFICEHOLDER?

1. THE UNIVERSITY ADMINISTRATOR

At the outset I must confess that these remarks will have less generality than I could wish. I agreed to lecture on the administrator. I find that I am about to lecture almost entirely on the university administrator. I have spent more than half my life in university administration, and none of it in any other kind. The longer a university administrator administers, the more he is impressed by the peculiarities of his calling. These peculiarities are such that the administrator of any other enterprise can learn little from the study of university administration; and the administrator of a university, for whom these peculiarities have a kind of morbid fascination, has little to say about the administration of an enterprise which is without them.

The business executive, for example, has a kind of authority within the business which is denied the university administrator. It is true that signs are now appearing that business may eventually be organized like a university, with the staff claiming a kind of academic freedom, participating in the formation of policy, and enjoying permanent tenure. When that happens, the university administrators of America will derive a certain grim satisfaction from watching the struggles of those captains of industry who have had the habit of complaining about the mismanagement of universities. But I fear that this will not be soon.

The university administrator is more like a political leader than any other kind of administrator. But even here the differences are, perhaps, more important than the similarities. The principal instruments of the American political leader are his party and his patronage. We cannot imagine his functioning at all without them. Both these instruments are quite properly denied the university administrator.

In this lecture it will appear that the task of the administrator is to order means to ends. I shall hope first to display the administrator at work with the means, and shall try to suggest the qualities that are required for the performance of his duties in regard to them, whether or not the end is clear, correct, or given. I shall then pass to the administrator at work with the end, the administrator who is seeking to define, clarify, or discover the aim of his institution. This is the highest function of the administrator. To perform it he needs all the qualities that are required for the disposition of means and, in addition, certain special, and very rare, abilities. The peculiarities of university administration relate both to the means and to the end. But the most difficult and most important problems are those which concern the end. I shall attempt to show the extraordinary significance of these problems at this moment in history. It is vital to civilization that university administrators face and solve these problems now.

Before I state what the qualifications of an administrator are, I should like to say that the mere statement of them will show that I do not possess them. I have been an administrator so long that I can tell you, I think, what an administrator ought to be. And this I can do even though I have never succeeded in being a good one myself. I discovered the things I know too late for them to be of use to me. There was nobody to give me this lecture when I began to administer. Even if there had been, it might not have helped much; for as Aristotle remarked, men do not become good by listening to lectures on moral philosophy.

But if I had known that I was going to be an administrator,

and if I had fully understood what the qualifications for the post were, I might have got a different education and tried to develop a different set of habits from those which I possess. One purpose of this lecture is to indicate the education and the habits which the prospective administrators should seek to acquire, so that they may perhaps be spared the remorse to which I am condemned.

The minimum qualifications of an administrator in his dealings with the means are four. They are courage, fortitude, justice, and prudence or practical wisdom. I do not include patience, which, we are told, President Eliot came to look upon as the chief requirement of an administrator. For reasons which will appear later, I regard patience as a delusion and a snare and think that administrators have far too much of it rather than too little.

I do not include temperance, which in the case of the administrator would be the habit of refraining from making decisions that should be made by his subordinates. This is a matter between administrators and should not be discussed before the uninitiated.

Nor do I include the theological virtues: faith, hope, and charity, though the administrator needs them more than most men. I omit them because they come through divine grace, and I am talking about what the administrator can accomplish by his own efforts. Since it is not within his power to obtain the theological virtues, I must leave him to work that he may deserve them and pray that he may receive them.

When I say that the administrator should have courage, fortitude, justice, and prudence, I am saying only that he should be a good man. If the administrator is to function at all, he must have prudence or practical wisdom, the habit of selecting the right means to the end. But the administrator's life reveals that, though the virtues may be separated for purposes of analysis, they are one in practice. The administrator cannot exercise prudence without courage, which is the habit of taking responsibility; fortitude, which is the habit of bearing the consequences; and justice, which is the habit of giving equal treatment to equals.

Habits are formed by action. The way to become a good

administrator is to administer. But this is also the way to become a bad administrator; for vice is a habit, too. The minimum function of the administrator is to decide, and, since he has to make more decisions than most men, he has the chance to be either an especially good or an especially bad man.

But you will say that most of the administrators you have known have not been especially good or especially bad men. This is because there are three courses, rather than two, open to the man who holds an administrative position. He can practice the four virtues I have named, he can practice their opposites, or he can decline to make decisions. Since the third is by far the easiest course, it is the one most administrators follow. I have known university presidents who have performed the almost superhuman feat of making no recommendations to their boards of trustees. I knew one who publicly took the view that the trustees made the decisions; he did not.

The administrator is a man who decides upon the class of cases committed to his care. If he fails to decide, he may be an officeholder; he is not an administrator. The shifts and dodges and downright dishonesty to which administrators will resort in the effort to become officeholders are an element of low comedy in the high tragedy of university administration. Lord Acton has familiarized us with the notion that power corrupts. He might have added a word or two on the corruption wrought by the failure to exercise authority when it is your duty to exercise it. The chairman of a department once told a university president that a member of the departmental staff was so inferior that he should leave the university, and two weeks later recommended that the same man be placed on permanent tenure at a large increase in salary. The reason, of course, was that he knew the president would turn down the recommendation. The president would bear the onus of blighting the hopes of the man in question, and the chairman could avoid the practice of the virtues. This came close to practising their opposites; for it was cowardly, pusillanimous, unjust, and unwise. But it is more charitable and more nearly describes the state of mind of this chairman to say that he merely decided that he did not want to administer. Administration was unpleasant, and he would leave it to the president.

Administration is unpleasant, as anything that requires the exercise of the virtues I have named must be. It is doubtful whether even these virtues can be exercised without divine aid. And the happiness which they give is not, I fear, a happiness in this life. The pressure upon a university administrator to become an officeholder is enormous. But there is an easy way of avoiding these troubles, and that is not to take the job. No man of mature years who accepts an administrative position in a university can claim that he did not know what his troubles would be. If there is such a man, he still has a way out; he can resign.

An air of martyrdom is unbecoming to the administrator. If he stays in office he has only himself to blame, and his failures will always be his own fault. They will result from his lack of moral stamina or mental capacity, or from his neglect of Bismarck's dictum that politics is the art of the possible. What is possible in any given situation depends to some extent on the material resources at the administrator's disposal, but far more on the abilities and spirit of his constituency. The administrator may make the wrong appraisal of his material resources or of the abilities and spirit of his constituency. He may overestimate his power to enlarge his material resources or to enhance the abilities and spirit of his constituency. If he is mistaken in any of these particulars, he has attempted the impossible and deserves to fail. If he fails, he should resign. He should not become an officeholder.

The administrator who is willing to be an administrator and not merely an officeholder will find that the strain is chiefly upon his character, rather than his mind. Administration is a work of the mind, because it is ordering the means to the end, and the principle of order is the intellect. Prudence or practical wisdom is a habit of the practical intellect. It involves knowledge of the available means and some rational notion of the effectiveness of the available means to promote the end in view. But such knowledge is not difficult to come by, and much of what passes for administrative knowledge is not knowledge at all. Knowledge is not information. The characteristic of knowledge is organization. There are few principles of administration, and they are simple and easy.

Prudence cannot be taught any more than courage, fortitude, or justice can be taught. You can be told what these things are. You can be shown examples of their exercise. But you develop courage, fortitude, and justice by practicing them, and so you develop prudence, too. I do not minimize the intellectual difficulties involved in reaching an important practical decision. I merely say that these difficulties are of such a nature that previous formal instruction will do little to assist in their solution, and that, compared with the strain on the character that administration of the means carries with it, the strain on the mind is insignificant.

The strain on the character is very great. The administrator who is afraid of anybody or anything is lost. The administrator who cannot stand criticism, including slander and libel, is lost. The administrator who cannot give equal treatment to equals is lost. In a university he must give equal treatment to equals no matter how much it would promote his plans or assuage his feelings not to do so. I would recommend to the young members of the faculty of any university that they attack the administration. Their advancement will then be assured; for the administration will have to lean over backward to show that these attacks did not prevent a fair appraisal of the professors' scholarly contributions.

The administrator has all these ways to lose, and he has no way to win. Almost every decision an administrator makes is a decision against somebody. This is true even of decisions that look as though they were for somebody, like a decision to raise a man's salary. The administrator quickly learns that such a decision is really a decision not to raise the salaries of other men in the same department. In a university the administrator must appeal for support to those whom he has alienated in the course of his duty. Some idea of his situation may be obtained by asking what sort of co-operation the President of the United States would get from Congress in his second term if he had had the duty, and had conscientiously performed it, of fixing the salary and rank of each member of that body for four years. If the administrator were a judge, he could expect the litigants to go away and leave him alone after he had reached his decision. As an administrator he must expect that those whom he has decided against will remain with him and view his labors as something less than inspired.

The natural course, then, is to become an officeholder. Your life will be much easier, and you may even become popular. To the administrator, the university often seems like a gigantic conspiracy to turn him into an officeholder. The trustees have accepted membership on the board because it is an honor. They are interested and pleased as long as the institution is prosperous—and peaceful. An administrator who administers is bound to cause trouble. Administrative decisions affect the lives, the fortunes, and even the sacred honor, of members of the faculty. An administrator who wants the support of the faculty will make as few decisions as he can. He will try to develop automatic rules covering all subjects to avoid the embarrassment which decisions on individual cases must cause him. In regard to new appointments he will seek to escape responsibility by appointing committees to advise him. He will resort to every undercover technique he can think of in order to have it appear that he did not make the decision, even when he did.

The chairman of the committee of the trustees to select a president for an important college on the Atlantic seaboard telephoned me the other day to inquire about one of my friends. He asked whether he was a good administrator. In my innocence, thinking he wanted a good administrator as president of his college, I entered upon a glowing description of my friend's administrative abilities. I found that my tribute was received without enthusiasm at the other end of the wire, and asked if I had misunderstood the question. "No," replied the trustee. "You understood the question, all right. But you are giving the wrong answer. You see, our retiring president was a very bad administrator. Our faculty likes that, and they are afraid of any successor who will be better."

There are few sins of omission in administration, at least in university administration. Since the administrator's salary, prestige, and perquisites are high, he will be criticised under any conditions. But he will seldom be seriously disliked if he does nothing. People will say that he is a weak man and that he does not give the institution the leadership it should have. But everybody secretly yearns for the days of Coolidge, and academic communities, whatever their protestations to the contrary, really prefer anarchy to any form of government.

The temptation, of course, is to bury yourself in routine. There is so much routine—so many reports, so many meetings, so many signatures, so many people to see—all of some value to the institution, that you can conscientiously take your salary and never administer at all. You can spend your entire time doing things that any $30-a-week clerk could do better and go home at night exhausted to report to your wife that you have had a hard day wrestling with university problems. The administrator who is determined to administer will find that the strain on his character is very great.

The strain on his mind results not so much from the intellectual difficulty of his problems as from his inability to command the time, assuming the ability and the willingness, to think. A university administrator has at least five constituencies: the faculty, the trustees, the students, the alumni, and the public. He could profitably spend all his time with any one of the five. What he actually does, of course, is to spend just enough with each of the five to irritate the other four.

The administrator who wants to administer will find that he cannot put in his time to the best advantage. On the one side are those things which are inevitable and urgent. On the other are those things which are important. The administrator should be devoting himself to those things which are important. But by definition he must devote himself to those which are inevitable and urgent. The question whether an assistant professor should have an increase in salary of $250 is not important, at least in an institution which has a deficit of one million dollars, which every well-regulated university should have. A deficit of $1,000,250 does not differ significantly from one of $1,000,000. But this question must be settled, while more important questions are postponed, because an offer from another university must be accepted or declined, or because the budget must go to the trustees at a certain time. And it must be passed upon by the administrator ultimately responsible, because, though $250 is not important, the quality of the staff is.

The problem of time, at least in a university, is insoluble. The administrator should never do anything he does not have to do, because the things he will have to do are so numerous that he cannot possibly have time to do them. He should never do today what he can put off till tomorrow. He should never do anything he can get anybody to do for him. He should have the largest number of good associates he can find; for they may be able to substitute for him. But he should be under no illusions here. The better his associates are, the more things they will think of for him to do.

Such thinking as the administrator can do will derive its value, not so much from his extraordinary knowledge or intellectual capacity, as from his locus in the institution. Like the architect, his view encompasses the whole and the interrelations of the parts. He is likely to take a more detached view of the whole and its parts than any of the staff. Though he will not have much time to think, he can devote the time he has to thinking as objectively as possible about the whole. He has the knowledge, the position, and the duty to do so.

He has this duty in relation to all the means at the disposal of the institution. In a university, for example, the curriculum is a means to the end of the institution. It is not ordinarily committed to the care of the administrator; he has not the authority to determine what the course of study shall be. But the curriculum is not a means, it is the chief means to the end of an educational enterprise. Nobody else has quite the opportunity which the administrator has to see the whole of the curriculum and the interrelations of the parts. The administrator fails in his duty, therefore, if he does not try to see from his point of vantage what the whole curriculum and its interrelations should be.

He must then try to induce those to whose care the curriculum has been committed to face the problems it raises as persistently, as seriously, and as impartially as possible. In this connection, too, the administrator must be a trouble-maker; for every change in education is a change in the habits of some members of the faculty. Nevertheless, the administrator must insist on the participation of the faculty in the constant reconsideration of the means which it is using to attain the end of the university; for his duty is not merely to decide upon the classes of cases committed to his care, but also to see to it that the other members of the community do not become officeholders in relation to the categories committed to theirs.

The task of the administrator in ordering the means is to keep the institution up to its own standards. These standards are a reflection of the end. The curse of universities is easy standards. For example, the relations among the members of the academic community are such that the failure to appoint or promote congenial men is bound to create much unpleasantness. The temptation to yield is very great; but, if the administrator yields in one instance, he must yield in more, and, before he knows it, a new and lower standard has been established, which is lowered in its turn by the same process. The commitments thus made by the administrator —and, whatever his virtues, he is bound to make some— gradually reduce his effectiveness and combine with the gradual alienation of his constituency to bring his usefulness to a close. The administrator has many ways to lose, and no way to win.

The remedy is a term, at the end of which the institution can decide once more whether it wishes to be managed by an administrator or ornamented by an officeholder. Failing some provision for the automatic termination of his services, the administrator must be in a perpetual mood of resignation, by which I do not mean mournful acceptance of the universe. I mean he must be perpetually prepared to get out. This solution is not ideal. Nobody will tell the administrator he should resign; this would be impolite, and finding a successor is very difficult. The administrator is usually the last person to know he should resign. He can always rationalize his salary, prestige, and perquisites into a burning conviction of his necessity to the institution. He is like a dub playing golf. He makes just enough good strokes to go on playing the game. But the chances are that the dub should give up golf and take to reading the Great Books.

How does the administrator or his constituency know whether his decisions are right or wrong? Since he is deciding upon the means to an end, his decisions are right or wrong depending on whether they help or hinder the institution in its effort to achieve the end. Where the end is simple and clear, the appraisal of the administrator is easy. If the end of an army is victory, a general who wins is good. If the end of a business is profit, an executive who makes money is good. But the measure of the statesman can be taken only in the light of some defensible conception of the end of the state, and the measure of a university administrator only in the light of some rational view of the end of the university.

The administrator cannot make the right decisions without some similar illumination. How can he decide on the means if he has no clear vision of the end? It is impossible for the administrator who understands the end to achieve it unless he has the character to select the right means, and impossible for him to select the right means unless he has the mind to understand the end. The difficulty of understanding the end of a university—and perhaps the lack of mind of university administrators—is suggested by the fact that the leading characteristic of educational institutions today is aimlessness.

The end of an institution gets lost as it matures. The enterprise goes on because it started and runs for the sake of running. If any other consideration than that of self-perpetuation is allowed to enter, it is usually that of prestige. Let us be famous for the sake of fame. We see a similar phenomenon in the case of states which have lost any conception of the end of political organization. They say, let us be powerful for the sake of power.

The fact that the purpose of universities is rapidly lost has led to the suggestion that they should be burned down every twenty-five years, or that the original faculty should consist of men forty years old, that no additions should be made, and that they should all retire at the age of sixty-five. These proposals seem drastic, but they are little more so than the facts demand. It is imperative to force the periodic reconsideration of the purposes of an institution.

The institution may have lost its usefulness at the end of twenty-five years. Its aim may have been accomplished. Or some other aim should, perhaps, be substituted for the original one. The University of Chicago, which I regard as the most useful institution in the world, is so because its original aim has been the subject of some reconsideration. The idea of the founders of this University was simply to establish a university in the Middle West, and one with Baptist overtones. Now there are many other universities in the region, and the Baptist overtones are almost inaudible.

The task of the administrator in a new enterprise is relatively easy, for there the purpose of the communal activity is clear and fresh in the minds of all the members of the community. Men are appointed to the staff because they are thought to be qualified for and interested in working toward the end. As the inevitable mistakes are made, as the vested interests harden, as the aim is changed to self-perpetuation, the difficulties of administration increase. The alteration takes place very rapidly. George Vincent, later president of the Rockefeller Foundation, who was a member of the first faculty of the University of Chicago, used to say that on the day the University opened, the faculty and students gathered in front of Cobb Hall and sang "Old Varsity" before the paint was dry. President Harper designed a new university, but his administrative autobiography makes depressing reading, because it shows how quickly a new institution congeals.

If the end of the institution has got lost, if the institution has congealed, if it suffers from the disease of aimlessness, then all the administrator's moral difficulties are intensified, and his mind undergoes serious strain. Now, in addition to summoning up the character necessary to select the right means, he must try to command the intelligence to discover the end. He must become a philosopher.

Men who possess and practice the virtues are rare enough.

Good men who are also good philosophers are rarer still. Good men who are good philosophers and who are willing to run the extraordinary occupational hazards, moral and mental, of university administration, are a race which appears to be extinct. Yet if I were asked what single thing American education needed most, I should reply that it needed such men; for the whole system of American education is losing itself in the wilderness for the lack of them. The academic administrators of America remind one of the French revolutionist who said, "The mob is in the street. I must find out where they are going, for I am their leader."

The president of a state university said recently that the object of his institution was to do whatever any important group in the state thought was useful. This amounts to saying that any important group in the state can determine the purpose of the university. The president in question took this view because it was easy, it was simple, and it would pay. He would not think himself; he established the fact that it was positively wrong for him to think; and the groups he was willing to have do his thinking for him would support the work which, they thought, it was the university's purpose to do.

This administrator merely stated explicitly what is implicit in the conduct of almost every American university. Almost every American university is managed in terms of the social pressures prevailing at a given time. Another state university president lately remarked that he was going to offer athletic scholarships because he could not get anything through the legislature with his present football team. Since the American university has been unable to formulate any idea of its function, its function is to do what any powerful group wants it to undertake. It has no standard by which to judge these requests, because it has no conception of the end. The modern university and the modern department store are therefore almost indistinguishable.

Anybody who has watched the development of the American university will have no difficulty in predicting that in the next twenty-five years it will greatly expand on the side of natural science, engineering, and the applied social sciences, such as business, industrial relations, and public administration. I have the greatest respect for all these subjects. Perhaps this is the direction in which the American universities should move. But I would point out that, if they do move in this direction, it is improbable that they will do so because they have considered the end and concluded that what civilization needs is more natural science, engineering, and applied social science. If they move in this direction, it is likely that they will do so because powerful pressures in society push them.

As it is easy and tempting to become an officeholder rather than an administrator, so it is easy and tempting not to think about the end. As everybody in the institution prefers an officeholder to an administrator, so everybody in the institution prefers not to be reminded that the university has, or should have, a purpose. The worst kind of troublemaker is the man who insists upon asking about first principles, and the first principle of any activity is the end. The last question that will be raised about a prospective academic administrator is whether he has any ideas. If it appears that he has, he is unlikely to be appointed, for he will rightly be regarded as a dangerous man. The situation in American education is much the same as that in American politics: the men who are needed most cannot be chosen; the qualifications to do the job disqualify the candidate for the post.

Yet somebody in the institution must think about the end; for otherwise the institution will get lost or fall to pieces. Our universities present an especially acute aspect of the general problem of the one and the many. A university should be one; but it is peculiarly a prey of centrifugal forces, which are always driving it apart. This is because no end has yet been discovered and accepted by the American university sufficiently clear to make sense of its activities, to establish a standard for criticizing them, and to unify those who are carrying them on. Even a mob will disintegrate if it does not know where it is going.

The administrator must accept a special responsibility for the discovery, clarification, definition, and proclamation of the end. But he does not own the institution. The administrator's responsibility is to get others to join him in the search for the end and to try to lead all his constituency to see and accept it when it has been found. He must conceive of himself as presiding over a continuous discussion of the aim and destiny of the institution. He must insist upon this discussion, and he must see to it that it never flags.

The difficulty is that the aim and destiny of an institution are not discovered by instinct or tradition; they must be arrived at by creative thought. For this, the administrator has neither the time, the atmosphere, nor the education which it demands.

It is suggestive that since Francis Bacon, who was, after all, a bad administrator and a bad man, no administrator who carried major responsibilities has published anything of any significance. In our own time, Hawthorne, Arnold, Trollope, and Mill have held administrative posts and done creative work. But Hawthorne was an officeholder, rather than an administrator, and the other three did not carry major responsibilities. Nor did any of them do any important thinking about the end of their administrative activity. There is little published evidence that any administrative officer has done so since Marcus Aurelius.

The end is the most important matter the administrator can deal with but its consideration can always be postponed; there is never any time for it. Though the administrator shares his lack of education with his contemporaries, associates, and fellow-citizens, they may be able to do something about their inadequacy in their leisure hours. The administrator's leisure hours are few, his administrative problems follow him home and plague his dreams, and his intellectual condition at the end of the day's work is such that he is barely able to cope with a detective story. The university administrator can force himself to do some reading and thinking by teaching; but this is bad for the students.

Yet Plato's answer to the question: What kind of administrators do states—and universities—require?, is valid for us today, after almost twenty-five hunded years. He said, "Unless either philosophers become kings or those whom we now call our kings and rulers take to the pursuit of philosophy seriously and adequately, and there is a conjunction of these two things, political power and philosophic intelligence, there can be no cessation of troubles, dear Glaucon, for our states, nor, I fancy, for the human race either."

Plato also tells us what kind of education is needed to produce the administrator we are seeking. Until the age of thirty-five, the candidate is to devote himself to his education, spending the last five years in the most profound metaphysical studies. Then for fifteen years he is to acquire practical experience in offices which Plato describes as those suitable to youth. The object is, of course, to develop the habit of practical wisdom, but even more to develop the moral virtues.

In Plato's words, "And in these offices, too, they are to be tested to see whether they will remain steadfast under diverse solicitations or whether they will flinch and swerve."

At the age of fifty, those candidates who have survived all tests and shown themselves the best in every task and every form of knowledge are ready to become administrators. But each will serve only for a limited term. The philosopher kings alternate between periods of philosophical study and administration, with the longer periods devoted to philosophy. When the turn comes for each, they toil in the service of the state, holding office for the city's sake, regarding the task not as a fine thing but as a necessity. As a reward for these sacrifices they depart eventually for the Islands of the Blest, and the state establishes public memorials and religious rites in their honor as though they were divinities, or at least divine and godlike men.

Plato was writing a utopia. Utopias are the products of desperate situations. They are constructed when everybody sees that nothing can be done, except perhaps to indicate the ideals toward which future generations should strive. We look to Plato not for the specifications of a practical program to be taken over intact, but for guidance in the formation by our own efforts of a practical program for our own day.

The essential points are that the administrator should not want to administer, but should be forced to do so for the public good; that he should have a long period of education, culminating in profound speculative study; that he should undergo a great variety of practical experience to form his character and develop the habit of practical wisdom; and that he should serve for a limited term, after which he should resume his studies, if he expects at some later time to have another. This is the kind of scheme which is called for if the administrator is to have the moral and intellectual qualities which the times demand.

You will say that even this reduced and denatured version of the Platonic program remains utopian still. It is a sufficient reply that our situation is so desperate that nothing not utopian is worth trying. We know that the world may at any moment burst into flames. We know that we can hope to save ourselves only by the most tremendous and well-directed efforts. Bewildered and tortured humanity should be able to look in this crisis to those institutions created to elevate the minds and hearts of men, to symbolize their highest powers and aspirations. To say of a university now that its object is to maintain itself or to preserve accepted values and institutions is to deny the responsibility imposed by the community on those privileged persons whom it has set apart to think in its behalf, to criticize its ways, and to raise it to its highest possible moral and intellectual level.

We can take one of two positions about education today. Either it aims to transform the minds and hearts of men, or it is completely irrelevant. Either it is almost our only hope or it is literally child's play, a way of keeping the young occupied until they can enter the army, which may be blown to bits without notice, or go to work in an economic system which is rapidly dissolving, or become citizens of a country and members of a civilization which—so we should have to tell them if we spoke frankly—are in the greatest peril in their history. Albert Einstein's estimate that in the next war two-thirds of the populations involved will be killed seems conservative, and who will say that there will not be a next war and that it will not be soon?

We know that agreements to control uranium deposits, to permit inspection of atomic-power plants and factories, to disarm, and even the solemn agreement which is the charter of the United Nations itself can last only so long as each of the participating members wants them to last. We know that a world government can arise only if the peoples of the world want it, and can endure only as there is a world community to support it. The prospects of a world civil war are not attractive.

We must have international agreements. We must work toward world government. But the significance of these agreements and of all efforts to frame a world constitution and get it adopted lies largely in the fact that all discussion of world unification may promote the community upon which such unification must rest. Such unification ultimately rests on the transformation of the minds and hearts of men.

If we must abolish war or perish, and if war can be abolished only by this transformation, then the aim of educational institutions is to bring about this transformation. And the task is one of terrifying urgency, so urgent that the triviality and frivolity of American education and the petty and selfish concerns of its leaders seem blasphemous as well as suicidal.

You may say that there is a disproportion between the end that I propose and the means that I have chosen. You may feel that there is little in the record of educational institutions in this country to suggest that, even if they devoted themselves wholeheartedly to the work, they could save civilization. If this is so, then we should take the enormous funds now devoted to the educational enterprise and use them to provide a few pleasant final hours for our starving fellow-men in Europe and Asia. The plight of mankind is such that if we seriously conclude that our activity is irrelevant to it we should give up the activity. The world cannot afford the luxury of so wasteful a monument to an abandoned dream.

As the minimum function of the administrator is ordering the means, so his highest function is discovering and clarifying and holding before his institution the vision of the end. As the qualifications for the administrator's minimum function are courage, fortitude, justice, and prudence, so the qualification for his highest function is philosophical wisdom. At this epoch in history we can demand nothing less of the administrator than this combination of practical and philosophical wisdom, with the moral qualities necessary to sustain it.

The reward of the administrator may not be public memorials, religious rites, and a pleasant journey to the Islands of the Blest. For these things he should care not at all. His satisfaction will come, even if he fails, from having seen and attempted one of the most difficult works of the mind and one of the most challenging human tasks.

April 23, 1946

2. THE ADMINISTRATOR RECONSIDERED: UNIVERSITY AND FOUNDATION

I should like to reflect upon the thirty-three years I have spent in the administration of corporations not-for-profit. At the outset I should like to reconsider my experience at the University of Chicago; it would then be appropriate to make some observations on the relatively new field of foundation administration; and finally I should like to refer to the problems that have arisen to plague the administrator in the years that have passed since first I sought to formulate my conception of the role and responsibility of the Administrator.

When I spoke at the University of Chicago on the administrator some ten years ago, I suggested that what the administrator needed was the moral virtues and a vision of the end to be achieved. I said that he had to have courage, fortitude, justice, and prudence, or, in sum, practical wisdom. I added: "I do not include patience, which we are told President Eliot came to look upon as the chief requirement of an administrator . . . I regard patience as a delusion and a snare and think that administrators have far too much of it rather than too little."

I must now confess that I believe Mr. Eliot was right, and I was wrong. I now think that my lack of patience was one of my principal disqualifications as an administrator.

I did not want to be an officeholder. I wanted, as the saying goes, "to get things done." This led me to push matters to a decision, sometimes by very close votes. One highly important resolution was defeated in the faculty by a tie. Under the rules of order I was permitted to vote, since the vote was by ballot. It turned out that the tieing ballot was cast by me. Representations were made from the floor that a decision on a central educational issue should not be reached by an evenly divided faculty. These representations I ignored; I had the votes I needed.

It is one thing to get things done. It is another to make them last. I was interested in effecting permanent improvements in American education, not in keeping the University of Chicago in an uproar. I should have known that the existence of a large and embittered minority, which felt that fundamental alterations of the University and its program had been pushed through without consideration of its point of view, destined such alterations to endure only until the minority could muster the strength to become the majority. The example of the College of Cardinals, who, I understand, never decide anything unless the vote is unanimous, and of the Quakers, who continue their discussion until consensus is reached, suggests the procedure that makes durability likely.

I followed this counsel of patience with the administrative group of the University, a gathering of twenty-three that met every two weeks. We never did anything without unanimous agreement. In one case, when it was decided that members of the faculty should receive decent salaries and turn their outside earnings over to the University, there were, as I remember it, sixteen long meetings before all objections were answered and all amendments disposed of one way or another.

I believe I should have done the same thing with the faculty representatives, who, under the constitution of the University of Chicago, have final power over all educational changes. If I had, I would have accomplished fewer things, but they might have survived longer. Of course, the price of such survival could well have been that I might not have lasted as long as I have—I might have died long since. As I said ten years ago, "The problem of time . . . is insoluble. The administrator should never do anything he does not have to do, because the things he will have to do are so numerous that he cannot possibly have time to do them. He should never do today what he can put off till tomorrow. He should never do anything he can get anybody to do for him. He should have the largest number of good associates he can find; for they may be able to substitute for him. But he should be under no illusions here. The better his associates are, the more things they will think of for him to do." The pressure of time is so great, the number of people who have to be convinced is so large, interminable discussion of the same subject with the same people is so boring, that the amount of patience a university administrator must have passes the bounds of my imagination, to say nothing of those of my temperament. But I have learned at last, or I think I have, that the university president who wants *durable* action, not just action, must have patience, and have it in amounts equal to the durability desired.

Considerations such as these have led me to think that if I had it to do over again I might have begun at Chicago in 1929 with a proposal for the reorganization of the University more basic than any I ever advanced. I now believe that the existing structure is impossible; the administrative task cannot be performed. I also believe that the departmental system, even when mitigated by large groupings like those at Chicago, tends to self-defeating excesses in specialization, self-defeating in the sense that the specialist who knows nothing outside his specialty eventually cannot succeed even in it. He becomes immune to ideas that might illuminate his labors. He cannot talk to those outside his specialty, because they cannot understand him, and he cannot understand them.

Chicago did take an important step, perhaps the most important that can be taken, when it established the College and insisted that the student could not specialize until he had had some taste of liberal education. This was intended to enable him to communicate later on with persons who had a different specialized education from his own, and it was even hoped that the liberal education he received would induce him to continue indefinitely an intellectual life outside his specialty. But the absorption of students and teachers in their own fields is such that basic liberal education is not enough: it cannot survive the pressure of specialized interests.

The impossible size of American universities and the lamentable extremes to which specialization has been carried lead me to believe that I should have proposed the reorganization of the University of Chicago on the lines of Oxford and Cambridge. The University should have been reconstituted into a federation of colleges, each representing among its students and teachers the major fields of learning. These colleges should have begun their work with the junior year, resting on the foundation of the College of the University, which terminated its work at the end of the sophomore year. That college was intended to be the equivalent of the humanistic *gymnasium* or the *lycée* or the British public school. The change would have meant that basic liberal education would have been followed by compulsory communication with the representatives of disciplines other than one's own throughout the whole educational process, and, in the case of teachers, throughout their lives.

Such colleges, with two hundred and fifty students and twenty-five faculty members, would be of manageable size. Each one would have an administrative officer who could be expected to lead the way to improvements, both numerous and lasting. The University as a whole should not have a permanent, full-time head. The ceremonial, representative functions of the university president could be performed, as at Oxford and Cambridge, by a temporary official.

The only objection I can think of to this proposal is that there would be no president to raise money for the University. A university president or ex-president cannot be expected to have much sympathy with this objection.

The adoption of the Oxford and Cambridge organization might suggest to the American universities the advantage of one or two other aspects of higher education in the United Kingdom. The abolition of the credit system and the substitution of a program of external examinations would do more than any other single thing to make American universities into educational institutions. The reduction of the periods of formal instruction to twenty-four weeks a year, on which the Chicago faculty defeated me by an overwhelming vote—it was as though they had voted to refuse a salary increase of 25%—would give impetus to research, prolong the lives of teachers, and throw the responsibility of education where it belongs, upon the students. But this is by the way. The main point is that administration by persuasion and agreement, which is the only kind that brings lasting results, cannot be conducted in the vast chaos of the American university, and that the remedy for it, federalization, would also remedy that mutual deafness which specialization has made the characteristic disease of the higher learning in America.

With these important alterations and reservations, I am ready to stand on my lecture of ten years ago about the administration of universities. What about the administration of foundations, in which I have now spent almost five years? At first glance they seem like paradise for the university administrator. Foundations have no faculty, no students, no alumni, and no football team. The president of a foundation does not have to spend all his waking hours plotting how he can raise money. The Lord Chancellor of Gilbert and Sullivan said, "In my court I sit all day, giving agreeable girls away." Substitute millions for girls and you have the life of a foundation executive as it seems to a university president who has never been a foundation executive.

When one is a foundation executive one begins to appreciate certain things about universities that are not always in one's ungrateful mind when one is administering a university. The academic tradition is so attenuated in this country that the administrator of an academic institution is likely to feel that it does not exist. His preoccupation with his trustees is likely to be such that he does not notice the functioning in the university of what John K. Galbraith has called "countervailing power." In a foundation, where there is no tradition yet and where there is no countervailing power, the administrator may recall with some nostalgia that the academic tradition did to some extent protect the academic enterprise and that the tension among administration, faculty, trustees, students, alumni, donors, and the public did have a tendency to keep any group from totally destroying the independence of the academic body.

It is true that the academic body has been in serious danger of losing its independence. The reason is that nobody can understand why it should have it. And the reason why nobody can understand this is that the colleges and universities of this country have, in their desire for popularity and money, gladly responded to every pressure and every demand. They have insisted on their dependence; they have become folk institutions, reflecting the whims, no matter how frivolous or temporary, of those whose support they hope to gain.

Where the academic tradition is stronger than it is in the United States and better understood by the population, it is effective even in restricting the use of the powers that trustees and ministers of education can legally exert. In England, Scandinavia, and Holland, for example, the legal powers of political officers and lay trustees, which equal those of their American counterparts, are never exercised in academic matters.

Weak as the academic tradition is in America, it still exists. But there is not and never has been any tradition that suggests what is proper or improper in the management of organized philanthropy. Formal restraints are imposed on the trustees of foundations by law, but the law is far from clear. Moreover, though the law may point out what you should not do, it does not purport to tell you what you should do. We know that a foundation cannot retain its exemption from taxation if it finances the campaign of a candidate for political office. The law does not tell us whether the best use of a foundation's money is to finance a study of the way in which bees tell distance, though we do know that such a grant, if made to a university rather than a private beekeeper, is not likely to endanger the tax exemption of the foundation.

Let me take an example that shows that not even the rudiments of a coherent attitude, much less a tradition, about foundations yet exist. It might have been supposed that the foundations would be regarded as the finest flower of free enterprise. The policy of the country has been to encourage people to finance religious, charitable, educational, and scientific endeavor through private contributions rather than through taxes. This policy appears in the steadily expanding provisions for exempting these contributions from taxation. In some countries such exemptions are difficult, if not impossible, to obtain. We rightly regard this result as reflecting the socialistic leanings of those countries. They want the state in charge of everything.

Yet critics of the foundations in this country, who represent the extreme right wing of American politics, and who are constantly in full cry against all efforts to extend the scope of governmental action, have repeated over and over again, with the evident intention of getting it accepted as an axiom, the proposition that tax-exempt money is "the public's" money. This means that detailed governmental supervision of the foundations is necessary: the government must see to it that "the public's" money is properly spent.

If this proposition is correct, it would seem to apply to all tax-exempt institutions. If a congressional committee may follow every foundation grant and analyze the thoughts of its recipient, then congressional committees may presumably check on "the public's" money when it supports preachers and teachers and seek to analyze (and control) their thoughts as well.

It has hitherto been thought that tax-exemption was conferred for the purpose of facilitating the performance of public tasks by private agencies. For example, a corporation that carries on education and research to that extent relieves the taxpayers of their obligation to finance such work. Tax-exemption can impose no duty on colleges and universities except that of conducting teaching and research according to their best judgment of what good teaching and research are. It cannot impose the duty of making sure that the teaching and research conform to the views of a majority of a legislative committee.

The powers of Congress to decide on the class of corporations that may be exempt from taxation are undoubted. An attempt by that body, or any other governmental agency, to go beyond the decision that a corporation is engaged in *bona fide* charitable, religious, educational, or scientific work and to decide that it ought to engage in or finance only such preaching, teaching, and investigation as the government may from time to time approve clearly violates the long established policy of this country, and, in my opinion, violates the First Amendment as well.

In my Chicago lecture I said, "The temptation, of course, is to bury yourself in routine. There is so much routine—so many reports, so many meetings, so many signatures, so many people to see—all of some value to the institution, that you can conscientiously take your salary and never administer at all. You can spend your entire time doing things which any $30-a-week clerk could do better and go home at night exhausted to report to your wife that you have had a hard day wrestling with university problems. The administrator who is determined to administer will find that the strain on his character is very great."

In foundation work the refuge of the administrator is frittering, rather than routine, though there is plenty of that, too. The administrator of a foundation has to have a vision of the end, and, in the light of it, has to decide what expenditure is most likely to achieve it. He must decide that for the purposes of his foundation A is better than B, that X University is better than Y University, and he must do this though B is more influential than A and Y more celebrated than X. The temptation, of course, is to recommend that both A and B, both X and Y, receive some money and thus to get the best of both worlds by combining popularity and effectiveness.

Most foundations, unlike the Fund for the Republic, have very general purposes, such as the welfare of mankind. The decision as to what expenditures will promote the *real* welfare of mankind is so difficult, involving such tremendous intellectual effort, which can yield at best an approximating guess, that the easy way out is to give nearly everybody something for nearly everything in the hope that some interesting entries will emerge for the annual report.

The foregoing formula will not protect one today if support, no matter how little, is given to somebody who is unpopular, or to an unpopular cause. It is in the light of this situation that I approach the closing theme of my remarks. What has happened to the administration of corporations not-for-profit in the last ten years? In the Chicago lecture I said: "The administrator who is afraid of anybody or anything is lost. The administrator who cannot stand criticism, including slander and libel, is lost." This is still true. I went on: "The natural course, then, is to become an officeholder." But even being an officeholder will not protect you now. The great change that has taken place in recent years is a change in the atmosphere in which the administrator must function. It is at present an atmosphere of suspicion and fear.

Since the clouds of suspicion and fear have rolled in, along with rising costs, those corporations not-for-profit which have to raise money, as all colleges and universities think they must, have felt constrained to propitiate those forces which have generated fear and suspicion or those persons and groups who have been influenced by it. Those corporations not-for-profit which do not have to raise money have felt constrained to merge innocuously into the environment by veering off from any activity or from any association that could be criticized.

When the National Commander of the American Legion can call upon his comrades, of whom I am one, not to have anything to do with the Fund for the Republic, you can see what occupational hazards are connected with being an officer of a foundation. But then, Senator McCarthy called Harvard a "smelly mess," so perhaps I am no worse off now than when I was a university president.

Think what has happened of late to the great American principle that a man is to be judged by what he does, not by what he thinks, not even by what he says, certainly not by what his relatives think or say or even by what they do, surely not by what his acquaintances or acquaintances of his acquaintances think, say, or do. Since the country is full of organizations to which many people belong who have little understanding of what is actually going on in the organizations, it was long thought that mere membership in an unpopular organization did not necessarily show that an individual member subscribed to all the views to which other members might subscribe.

The Supreme Court, producing five opinions in a six to

two decision, has held that the First Amendment does not prevent Congress from narrowing the traditional limits of freedom of speech. The loyalty-security program of the government and the Attorney-general's list have been used to debar persons from public and private employment against whom nothing worse could be said than that they had associated with their mothers. Though the Fifth Amendment is simply another way of saying that the prosecution must prove its case by gathering evidence to sustain it, the use of the Amendment by one whose political views are in question is regarded as irrefutable justification of the charge.

What has happened to the great American principle that the chief qualification for a job is the ability to perform it? In almost no case that I can think of, from the Hollywood Ten to the teachers recently suspended in New York, has it been suggested that the alleged political views of the individual had any effect upon his work. The question of competence is never raised.

The object of universities, hospitals, and foundations is not the preservation of the status quo. It is the improvement of the conditions of human life and the clarification of its aims. A university that does not try to improve the educational system and the environment in which it operates, a hospital that does not try to improve medical practice, a foundation that is not dedicated to the welfare of man, is a failure. Yet universities, hospitals, and foundations that do these things must inevitably engage in criticism of existing practices, and if they do they must expect to be criticized in turn.

They will be "controversial." As Mr. Fulton Lewis, Jr. has so well said, "Controversy is the lifeblood of American society." But such a statement usually turns out to have little meaning when a controversial person is in question. How often have we heard of people of undoubted loyalty like Bishop Oxnam and the American Civil Liberties Union being denied the privilege of speaking or meeting because they are controversial! How do you become controversial? By being attacked, and it makes no difference how innocent you are or how silly, stupid, or irresponsible the attack may be. It will be remembered that Bishop Oxnam was refused permission to speak in the Philharmonic Auditorium in Los Angeles after he had been "cleared," as the saying goes, by the House Un-American Activities Committee. The principal attack upon the American Civil Liberties Union was delivered by the most disreputable of the various State Un-American Activities Committees, the Tenney Committee of California.

The winds are shifting. The demise of Senator McCarthy, the bi-partisan vote for a commission to look into the loyalty-security programs, the apologies distributed by various agencies of the government to persons wronged by mistake or by frivolous or perjured testimony, the judicial decisions and the changes in regulations affecting passports, the improvement of the procedure of congressional investigations—all these things may encourage those who believe that we do not have to jettison our liberties in order to protect them. Mr. Truman would have been impeached if he had proposed that the Russians fly over our country and photograph our military installations. He had a bad time because he once said that he liked Old Joe; but his successor could correspond with Zhukov, and Vice-president Nixon has felt free to say that one of the most important results of the Geneva conference was the establishment of friendly personal relations between the Russian leaders and President Eisenhower. As the wind blows now, those who believe that universities are centers of independent thought and that foundations are accumulations of venture capital dedicated to pioneering are doing fairly well. But irremediable harm was done to these conceptions in the last wind, because the timidity that it created lingers on.

And what about the next wind? The administrator ought to have a vision of the end that is clear and true regardless of meteorological conditions.

It is not merely inevitable that we are different and have different views; it is desirable that this should be so. From the clash of opinion truth emerges, and the human race advances.

Hence the essence of Americanism is discussion. It is not name calling or suppression. It is certainly not dogma or prejudice. The only political dogma in America is that discussion is the road to progress, that every man is entitled to his own opinions, and that we have to learn to live with those whose opinions differ from our own. After all, they may turn out to be right.

The administrator must have a clear, true vision of the end, and he must have courage, fortitude, justice, prudence, and patience in order to pursue it through all kinds of weather. The administrator who instead of pursuing the end pursues public relations may make himself and his institution rich and popular. Public relations means trying to find out what the prevailing opinion is before you act and then acting in accordance with it. The tendency of the pursuit of public relations is to make everybody think, look, talk and act like everybody else: how can anybody criticize you if you are like everybody else? The pursuit of popularity brings the kind of success that turns to dust and ashes in the administrator's mouth; it means that he and his institution have failed in reality, because the end has got lost, and so they have not done for their fellow-men what they were intended to do. The moral virtues and the vision of the end—these are still what the administrator needs; he needs them today as never before.

September 19, 1955

PART III: *THE FUND*

Introduction: FREEDOM AND THE FUND

The National Press Club asked me to speak about the report
of the Reece Committee on foundations. The American Veterans' Committee in Washington asked me to speak about
the Fund for the Republic. The publisher of this book asked
me to write a special article for it about the Fund and its
future.

I complied with these requests because I thought the subjects were important, though not equally so. The Reece Committee was not unimportant; but the lessons it taught were
not precisely those in which it set out to give instruction. It
shed more light on the possible peculiarities of congressional
investigations than on the successes and failures of foundations. Foundations are a special American phenomenon; the
people ought to know about them. It is not easy to learn anything worth knowing about them from the Reece report. But
in spite of those elements of fantasy which make the report de-
lightful summer reading, the Reece report had an intimidating effect on the officers and trustees of foundations, a group
that was fairly cautious to start with. This is the principal importance of the report.

The speech before the American Veterans' Committee was
an account of the work of the Fund as I saw it at the time.
The special essay written for this book about the Fund is a

statement of what I think about the Fund now. I should emphasize that these are both purely personal expressions: I have not discussed either of them with any members of the Board of Directors. That Board sets the policies of the Fund, and does so in great detail and in the most careful and painstaking manner. The opinions set forth in these two pieces are those of one director.

ONE

THE FUND, FOUNDATIONS, AND THE REECE COMMITTEE

These remarks have been written for myself alone, and not on behalf of the Fund for the Republic, the Directors of which I have not consulted; nor for the Ford Foundation, of which the Fund for the Republic is completely independent; nor for other foundations.

The foundations have been uncommonly vocal recently; they have also been uncommonly unanimous. I have been dealing with the foundations in one way or another for more than thirty years. They have always been distinguished by their lack of fellow feeling. They have scorned a project if it required the co-operation of another foundation. It is therefore one of the more absurd charges of the Reece Committee that the foundations were an intellectual cartel. The Reece Committee forced them to huddle together in self-defense. One more investigation and they might become a cartel.

The conduct of the majority, if it was the majority, of the Reece Committee was so scandalous that it outraged almost all the press and apparently even one of its own members. At any rate, Angier L. Goodwin of Massachusetts wrote a new kind of concurring opinion, one that disagreed with all the conclusions of the opinion with which it purported to concur. In the conduct of the hearings Mr. Reece added some new wrinkles to the distortions that we have become accustomed to in congressional investigations.

The foundations were elaborately attacked by the staff and by some witnesses of dubious standing. Then, pleading that Mr. Hays of Ohio would not let him conduct the hearings as they should be conducted, Mr. Reece adjourned them and informed the foundations that they could file written statements. Perhaps the most depressing fact about the report of the so-called majority of the Reece Committee is that Mr. Reece takes credit for relieving the foundations of what he calls the "embarrassment" of cross-examination. You might as well execute an innocent man without the embarrassment of a hearing. If you did, however, nobody would have the affrontery to claim that you had conformed to the principles of Anglo-American jurisprudence.

The most entertaining of the new wrinkles was that the majority of the Committee took a philosophical position. The Cambridge ladies, e. e. cummings said, lived in furnished souls; so Mr. Reece and Mr. Wolcott came bustling out in second-hand suits of anti-empiricism, supplied them by the sages of the staff. Mr. Reece and Mr. Wolcott were much against empiricism, which they associated with moral relativism, irreligion, the cultural lag and ultimately with subversion.

The Congressmen could not be bothered with history. They overlooked the fact that some of the most empirical empiricists in history, like Hume and Montaigne, were thoroughgoing tories. The Congressmen could not be bothered with consistency: for example, they went after the teachers' colleges for sponsoring empiricism and then after the Fund for the Advancement of Education for not sponsoring the teachers' colleges.

If a committee may charge a foundation with empiricism, why not charge a college with it, and if with empiricism why not also with Presbyterianism or Catholicism or any other philosophy, religion, or dogma that the committee does not care for? The grant of tax exemption may carry with it certain obligations, and those who accept it may by implication agree that they must perform certain services. But it has never been supposed that by taking tax exemption a college, university, church, or foundation, otherwise within the law, was liable to condemnation because of the philosophy that it held. If there is such liability, the way is open to the most flagrant violation of religious freedom and of freedom of speech and teaching.

The lesson the majority, if it is a majority, of the Reece Committee wants to teach the foundations is stated in words of crystalline clarity: "They should be very chary of promoting ideas, concepts and opinion-forming material which run counter to what the public currently wishes, approves and likes."

Here the Committee throws overboard the principle accepted by the Cox Committee that the justification of the foundations is that they supply risk or venture capital in the field of philanthropy. That is what they are for, to take chances, the Cox Committee said. The Reece Committee would confine them to what a public relations man, presumably by a series of careful polls, found that the public currently wished, approved, and liked. The way to be safe would be to attract no attention, arouse no discussion, create no controversy.

Even this would not be enough. All the things of which the Committee now complains were currently wished, approved, and liked at the time the foundations did them. To meet the test laid down by the Committee, therefore, a foundation would have to be able to foresee what would become unpopular by the time of an investigation.

But even this is not enough. The issue is not what the public will wish, approve, and like. There is no evidence, for example, that the American public dislikes empiricism. Quite the contrary. The public does not dislike empiricism: the Reece Committee does, or rather two members of it do, or perhaps just the staff of the Reece Committee does. Running a foundation on these terms becomes an extra-hazardous occupation fraught with dangers that test pilots and submarine explorers and others who are up against nothing worse than the laws of Nature do not encounter.

The Reece Committee achieved some of its gaudiest ef-

fects by the simple process of giving old words new defini-
tions and then pinning the old words on the foundations.
This is the way that empiricism becomes subversive. Subversion now means, the Committee says, a promotion of
tendencies that may lead to results that the Committee will
not like. Hence support of the New Deal could be subversion. Social engineering, planning, world government, the
United Nations, William James, John Dewey, the American
Friends Service Committee, Dr. Kinsey and reform are all
subversive in the bright new lexicon of the Reece Committee. And of course all these things are socialistic, if not com-
munistic, too.

At times one feels when reading the report that old scur-
rilous words will be redefined and applied to any expression
of decent human feeling. So it was that a staff member found
himself identifying certain Papal Encyclicals as communis-
tic.

But the Reece report is said to be a majority report, and it
will be referred to in the future as a majority report. Its appendix will be quoted as an authoritative collection of dangerous names. The only reason for the appendix is to enable
some committee in the future to say of somebody that he was
listed by the Reece Committee. This fact will then be
greeted with hushed and incredulous awe by those to whom
it is communicated.

All you have to do to qualify for the appendix is to favor
world government or get mentioned by the *Daily Worker*.
The principal charge against one distinguished professor is
that he is quoted, apparently with approval, in a dissenting
opinion in the Circuit Court of Appeals. A low of some sort
is reached with the mention in the appendix of the name of
George F. Kennan. He is accused of the following—and this
is the total record—: a book of his was reviewed (we are not
told whether favorably or unfavorably) in the *Daily People's
World* and the *New World Review;* on May 9, 1950, the
New York *Times* reported that he spoke on Communist
China (what he said does not appear); and on May 28,
1950, the New York *Times* reported that he "attacked witch-
hunting of Communists." On the basis of such information

Mr. Kennan will in the future be referred to as "cited by the Reece Committee."

The appendix of the Reece Committee's so-called majority report is an endless carnival of good clean fun—it is almost two hundred pages long; but I must pass on. I cannot regard the Reece Committee as having more than symbolic or symptomatic importance. Its wild and squalid presentation affords a picture of the state of our culture that is most depressing. Its aims and methods are another example of the exploitation of public concern about Communism and subversion to further political ambition and to work off political grudges.

We may as well state it plainly: the Reece investigation in its inception and execution was a fraud. Nobody in his right mind could suppose that the great accumulations of wealth left by our richest men were being intentionally used by their trustees to overthrow the institutions of this country. Hence the Reece Committee had to take another tack: the trustees were said to be so busy that they had to leave the foundations to officers who were often quite disreputable. Though this relieved the men of wealth and standing of the charge of being knaves, it did so only at the expense of charging them with being fools. Only fools could be so careless as to allow enormous sums entrusted to them for charitable purpose to be stolen away and lavished on the subversion of their country.

Congress may properly investigate the foundations and seek to arrive at general legislative policy concerning them. But the most important question to ask about any given foundation is whether it is one. Is it actually using its money for religious, charitable, educational, or scientific purposes? The First Amendment suggests that tax exemption should not be denied or revoked because the particular views of religion, education, or science held or promoted by the foundation are unpopular.

On the other hand, nothing in the Constitution requires that tax exemption must be accorded an organization, which though in outward form a foundation, is actually a tax dodge, or a public relations device, or a scheme to promote the personal interests of the donor. The test is public versus private purposes. The Government may properly inquire into this question, since the exemption is granted with a promise of performance. The appropriate forum for the determination of the question of performance would seem to be a court.

As Dr. Johnson used to say, we must clear our minds of cant. When we do, we see that in general the foundations have for many years been following the prescription laid down for them by the majority of the Reece Committee. This prescription is to try to avoid doing what is or may become unpopular. The failure of the foundations to be universally popular at all times is seldom caused by a spirit of reckless abandon or eager pioneering on their part. It is caused rather by the difficulties of predicting what will be popular or unpopular.

Who could have imagined that helping prospective teachers in Arkansas to get an education would have ever been regarded by anybody as exhibiting dangerous tendencies of mind? But when a foundation did this, it was criticized by teachers, businessmen, and newspapers in that State and was of course complained of by the Reece Committee. What would the Foundation have done in Arkansas if it had been possible to foresee the reactions that in fact occurred? I do not say that the grant would not have been made, but I would not bet on it; for the foundations have in varying degrees suppressed their ambition to provide risk capital in favor of a desire to have what are called good public relations, that is, to avoid unpopularity.

We know that the Attorney-General's list is an *ex parte* finding of guilt with no probative standing in law. But how many foundations would give money to an organization or even to an individual in an organization on the Attorney-General's list, however meritorious the project? Would we support organizations that allowed groups listed by the Attorney-General to meet in halls owned by them? If not, for an irrelevant reason, one that has nothing to do with the quality of the proposal, but that has a great deal to do with our popularity, we have made our peace with Reece.

We know that the most dreadful aspect of the current situation is the atmosphere of suspicion and of guilt-by-association in which we live. We ought to say that until a man or an organization has been condemned by due process of law he or it must be presumed innocent, and therefore individuals and organizations are not to be automatically denied support solely on the ground that they are associated with unpopular people. Yet how many foundations would give money for a good purpose to be well carried out by an organization which, though not on the Attorney-General's list, was supposed to have some Communist members or was vaguely reported to be dominated by Communists?

We have come a long way since Lord Macaulay, who said, "To punish a man because we infer from some doctrine he holds or from the conduct of others who hold the same doctrine with him that he will commit a crime is persecution and is in any case foolish and wicked."

Congressman Reece was scoffed at. It was agreed that his investigation was a farce. I think he had good reason to be satisfied with himself. I think he won. Without firing a single serious shot, without saying a single intelligent word, he accomplished his purpose, which was to harass the foundations and to subdue such stirrings of courage, or even of imagination, as could be found in them. As I have said, there were not many there when he came on the scene. Congressman Cox had been there before him. And even before Congressman Cox, the foundations were coming to limit their venturesome risk capital supplying to the natural sciences, medicine, technology, and long-term research. These fields are of great public benefit. They are also not controversial. If there ever was a foundation that was willing to be controversial, that was willing to take risks and to venture capital in areas about which people have strong prejudices, it learned its lesson by the time Cox and Reece got through. Who will venture now?

The pressures of our time produce strange contradictions, as in the case of the man who said that there were two things he hated, intolerance and Jews. Even those who understand what they are talking about are sometimes afflicted with a disease that often attacks intelligent people, a disease that gives them such satisfaction in what they say that they are blinded to the fact that it makes no difference.

The Houston *Post* did a wonderful job on the situation in the schools of that city, but the deputy superintendent, who was fired, has not been reinstated. We all smiled at the decision of the commandants not to permit West Point and Annapolis to debate the entry of Communist China into the UN and applauded Mr. Eisenhower's sensible observations. We went away feeling very good, forgetting that West Point and Annapolis are not yet to be permitted to debate the entry of Communist China into the UN. The Illinois Department of the American Legion has repented, I hear, of its brutality to the Girl Scouts; but the Girl Scouts revised their Manual as the Legion demanded. We were pleased to notice that Bishop Oxnam was "cleared" by the House Un-American Activities Committee; but he was not allowed to speak at the Philharmonic Auditorium in Los Angeles. We assert that the Fifth Amendment is one of the brightest stars in the crown of our liberties and proclaim the inalienable freedom of every man not to testify against himself, conveniently overlooking the fact that almost everybody who has declined to do so is now unemployed. We say that a security system that deprives us of the services of some of our ablest people is scarcely helping us to be secure; we regard this as a pungent remark. But Davies and Oppenheimer are not working for the Government. And what about Edward U. Condon, retiring President of the American Association for the Advancement of Science, who has been repeatedly cleared, but who, at the prospect of his fourth or fifth investigation, pronounced himself investigated out of public service? And now, after Reece, how many foundations do you suppose would be prepared to assist such a man?

The temper of the times appears to be such that the real victories go to those who are nominally defeated. The rather messy anti-Communist legislation adopted at the close of the last session of Congress in 1954 and the pious resolution passed by the Senate at the opening of the first session of 1955 must be regarded as real victories for a senator who was formally condemned by his colleagues but two months previously. So must the requirement imposed on every public speaker these days that he disavow any connection with Communism and attack the vicious conspirators in the Kremlin.

The newer orthodoxy is an odd thing. For example, it requires us to be against McCarthy, but not too soon or too much, not in such a way as to arouse too much animosity in too many of those who might have a different opinion. If, for example, we say that rumor and gossip are an inadequate basis on which to condemn a man or a group, we are told that of course we are right, but that in this case the rumor and gossip are so widely believed that people would think bad thoughts of us if we insisted on proof. So it comes to this: we must ourselves adopt an un-American attitude because if we don't we may be regarded as un-American by those who have an admittedly un-American attitude. We are all dedicated to the great American tradition, but the battle-cry of the Republic is, what will people say?

The motto of the Fund for the Republic is, feel free. At least that is what the officers tell one another it ought to be. This is, I believe, the essence of Americanism. Our ancestors came to this country because they wanted to feel free. They developed laws and institutions under which they and we could feel free. The Declaration of Independence, the Constitution, the Bill of Rights, the amendments extending the suffrage—these are expressions of the American conviction that everybody should feel free. The limits of this feeling or this freedom are not to be found in a formless fear of public opinion. On the contrary, public opinion is to grow and change through the free discussion of all points of view.

These ideas seemed so important to a new and inexperienced foundation, the Ford Foundation, that something more than two years ago it established the Fund for the Republic. The Foundation gave the Fund $15 million and turned it loose as an independent corporation, a wholly disowned subsidiary, with a self-perpetuating board of directors of its own. Its mandate from the Foundation was to try to strengthen the basic rights guaranteed by the Constitution and to "support activities directed toward the elimination of restrictions on freedom of thought, inquiry, and expression in the United States, and the development of policies and procedures best adapted to protect those rights in the face of persistent international tension." Those were the happy, carefree, pre-Reece days.

Somewhat later, after the organization of the Fund, its chairman, Paul G. Hoffman, said: "We propose to help restore respectability to individual freedom . . . Out of our discussions has come a preliminary conclusion that the attention of the Fund should at this time be concentrated in the following five areas, not necessarily in order of priority: 1. Restrictions and assaults upon academic freedom; 2. Due process and equal protection of the laws; 3. The protection of the rights of minorities; 4. Censorship, boycotting, and blacklisting activities by private groups; 5. Guilt by association."

By restoring respectability to individual freedom the Board means that it hopes to help Americans feel comfortable about feeling free. A board better calculated to bring about this result would be difficult to find; for the members are all comparatively respectable, comparatively free, and comparatively interested in helping other people to feel so. The mere existence of this board should take the Fund some distance on the way toward the restoration of respectability to individual freedom. You cannot belong to this board without believing in conscientious nonconformity as necessary to the growth and progress of individuals and states. The mere existence of this board serves as a reminder that intelligent, even important, people can and do believe this even yet.

The Fund has no other axe to grind than support of the traditional liberties of the American people. It does not seek to support them by trying to influence legislation. It attempts instead to disentangle the issues, and to promote rational discussion of them. It helped the American Bar Association to make up its mind on congressional investigations by financing the Association's committee on national security and individual rights. It assisted the League of Women Voters to stir up discussion of civil liberties among its members and among the members of other organizations. It aided Columbia University in the presentation of the theme of its bicentennial and supported the efforts of the National Citizens' Commission on the Public Schools to promote debate about the condition of public education, with special reference to academic freedom and racial discrimination.

If you are going to disentangle the issues that affect the traditional liberties of Americans, one of the first big ones that you have to try to get clear is Communism in the United States. Not a day passes without the most positive statements being made on this subject. Many of them disclose a total lack of authentic information, but they are nonetheless positive for all that. The Fund for the Republic has made the Communist record in this country available through the work done by Professor Sutherland of the Harvard Law School. Professor Stouffer of Harvard has completed a book called *Communism, Conformity, and Civil Liberties,* representing the results of a study financed by the Fund of the attitudes of Americans on these subjects. Professor Rossiter of Cornell, with a considerable staff, is now embarking on a comprehensive investigation of what the Communist party has amounted to in the United States and what it amounts to now. These three jobs together should help the American people to decide on the relative importance of Communism in this country and on the successes and failures of the methods that have been employed to deal with it.

One of the methods that has been employed to deal with it that has been severely criticized is the security-loyalty program of the Government. Many suggestions have been put forward calling for a study by distinguished and disinterested persons. The Association of the Bar of the City of New York has organized such a study, which has been financed by the Fund.

Since we do not want subversive influences to reach our children, we have instituted methods of assaying the patriotism of teachers. It is widely believed that they are ineffective and that they interfere with education by frightening the teachers off the discussion of some subjects. Professor Lazarsfeld of Columbia has undertaken to find out for the Fund whether or not these conditions do actually exist in the high schools, colleges, and universities of the country.

It is charged that in the effort to eliminate subversive influences in motion pictures, radio, and television we have allowed irrelevant and unsupported attacks, or attacks of little value, to deprive men and women of their livelihood. Unauthorized private persons are alleged to determine by obscure means the fate of those on whom these attacks are made. John Cogley, a former editor of *The Commonweal,* has finished an investigation of blacklisting in the entertainment industry for the Fund for the Republic.

Through the American Friends Service Committee, the Catholic Inter-racial Council of Chicago, the National Council of Churches, and the Southern Regional Council the Fund has been trying to do something about the rights of minorities. The Fund regards Negro housing as the next big issue in race relations and will shortly announce its plans with regard to it.

The Fund for the Republic is a kind of anti-absurdity fund, a fund for the law of contradiction, a fund to remind us that we can't have things both ways. We can't brag about the Bill of Rights and talk about Fifth Amendment Communists. We can't say that every man has the right to face his accusers and go on using what the Denver *Post* has called "faceless informers." We can't proclaim our devotion to due process of law and then deny it to people we don't like.

The Fund for the Republic is a sort of Fund for the American Dream. I do not think the Fund can make the American Dream come true; but perhaps it can help keep it alive and clear. Perhaps it can show where we are forgetting the dream as it once was dreamt and can point out those places, and they are numerous, where the progress toward the realization of the dream has surpassed our most expansive expectations. Who knows? Perhaps some day "what will people say?" will be replaced as the Battlecry of the Republic by "feel free."

January 26, 1955

TWO

SOME TRUTHS ABOUT THE FUND FOR THE REPUBLIC

It should be noted at the outset that the only other award I ever received was from the American Legion. It was from Chicago Post 170. Perhaps that post is a bunch of mavericks, but I prefer to regard it as more representative of the rank and file of the Legion than the kingmakers who met in Indianapolis are. I joined the Legion, after 35 years as an unattached and skeptical veteran, because of my admiration for the program of the Illinois Department under the leadership of Irving Breakstone. I was happy to learn that the National Commander endorsed this program in February last. I was sorry to see him cross himself up six months later by condemning the Fund for the Republic, which had financed the program he had endorsed. It is embarrassing to have one's commander make slips of this kind.

I am surprised that there should be any differences of opinion about the Fund for the Republic. They must result from misinformation. Or perhaps they arise out of that confusion which overtakes statesmen, columnists, and commentators in the hustle and bustle in which they perform their task of cleansing the Commonwealth of influences that threaten the positions on which they have built their reputations.

Congressman B. Carroll Reece, for example, who made his

reputation as chairman of a congressional investigation into foundations, announced, almost before the Fund was organized, that its object was to investigate congressional investigations. As a matter of fact, less than one percent of the Fund's expenditures have been devoted to this subject; and this money was spent through a committee of the American Bar Association, the report of which was adopted by a large majority of the House of Delegates at the meeting of the Association fourteen months ago.

In February, 1953, the Ford Foundation made a considerable grant to the Fund for the Republic, and the umbilical cord between them was severed. At that time the Board of Directors of the Fund made a public statement that said, "The major factor affecting civil liberties today, in our opinion, is the menace of Communism and Communist influence in this country. Coupled with this threat is the grave danger to civil liberties in methods that may be used to meet the threat. We propose to undertake research into the extent and nature of the internal Communist menace and its effect on our community and institutions. We hope to arrive at a realistic understanding of effective procedures for dealing with it.

"We regard the sphere of operation of the Fund as including the entire field of freedom and civil rights in the United States and take as our basic charter the Declaration of Independence and the Constitution . . .

"Out of our discussions has come a preliminary conclusion that the attention of the Fund should at this time be concentrated in the following five areas . . .

1. Restrictions and assaults upon academic freedom;
2. Due process and equal protection of the laws;
3. The protection of the rights of minorities;
4. Censorship, boycotting, and blacklisting by private groups;
5. The principle of guilt by association and its application in the United States today."

I call your attention to the fact that this statement was issued at a time at which I had no connection with the Fund. Of the original directors those who are still serving are

Paul G. Hoffman, Chairman of the Board; George N. Shuster, President of Hunter College, Vice-chairman of the Board; Charles W. Cole, President of Amherst College; Russell L. Dearmont, Attorney of St. Louis; Erwin N. Griswold, Dean of the Harvard Law School; William H. Joyce, Jr., Chairman of the Board, Joyce, Inc.; Meyer Kestnbaum, President, Hart Schaffner & Marx; M. Albert Linton, Chairman of the Board, Provident Mutual Life Insurance Co.; John Lord O'Brian; J. R. Parten, President, Woodley Petroleum Co.; Elmo Roper; Mrs. Eleanor B. Stevenson; and James D. Zellerbach, President, Crown Zellerbach Corporation.[1] They were later joined by Harry Ashmore,[2] Executive Editor of the *Arkansas Gazette;* Chester Bowles; and Robert E. Sherwood.[3] This group, which I have seen described as "left-wing", supervises the execution of the program announced by the Board two and a half years ago.

This program is just what it started out to be, no more, no less. But you would never guess it from some of the things you hear and read these days. For example, the Annual Report, which, by the way, is given away free to anybody who asks for it, shows that almost a third of the money appropriated up to the date of the Report had gone into race relations. The Catholic Interracial Council of Chicago, the Methodist Church, the National Council of Churches of Christ, the American Friends Service Committee, and the Southern Regional Council have received grants to assist them in the protection of the rights of minorities. One of the most serious problems those minorities face is that of housing. The Fund has established a commission on this subject headed by Earl B. Schwulst, President of the Bowery Savings Bank of New York, and including such men as Father John Cavanaugh of Notre Dame, Elliott Bell, of *Business Week;* Clark Kerr, Chancellor of the University of California at Berkeley; Stanley Marcus, of Neiman-Marcus; and Henry R. Luce of Time, Inc. Not even in the South has any responsible criticism of these activities appeared. In the criticisms of the Fund no mention of these activities appears.

For such conspiratorial agencies as the Congregational Christian Church, the Universalist Church, the YMCA, the

YWCA, the American Friends Service Committee, the League of Women Voters, the American Heritage Council, and Columbia University the Fund has appropriated approximately a quarter of a million dollars to help promote the discussion of the basic ideas and documents in American history and political theory; $50,000 of this is being used to bring the good news of these ideas and documents to my embattled comrades in the Illinois Department of the American Legion. Although these expenditures are set forth in detail in the Annual Report, which has been circulating for almost two months, I do not often hear or see them mentioned by those who think less well of the Fund than I do.

It may surprise those of you who derive your information from such sources to learn that the Fund has made grants to the Common Council for American Unity to expand its work in protecting the legal rights of aliens, to the University of Pennsylvania to study the interference of the Post Office Department with the flow of information and opinion, to the National Book Committee for a study of the right to publish and to read, and that it has assisted various bar associations and legal organizations that are trying to see to it that indigent and unpopular defendants are adequately represented by counsel.

Pursuant to its original resolution the Board of the Fund had devoted almost a third of its expenditures up to the date of the Annual Report to the study of various aspects of Communism in the United States. Professor Arthur E. Sutherland of the Harvard Law School directed the compilation of the first complete digest of the principal legal proceedings in which the Communist Party has been involved. Professor Samuel A. Stouffer of Harvard conducted a national opinion survey in order to discover what the attitudes of the American people toward Communists and radicals were. Professor Clinton Rossiter of Cornell, with the assistance of twelve experts and a large staff, is making the definitive study of what the Communist Party has amounted to in this country and what it amounts to now. The Stanford University Law School has received a grant to make an objective analysis and critical summary of the testimony of the principal witnesses in the most important Communist trials.

The professors who direct these studies have complete freedom. They are given the money and asked to recruit their own staffs and work out their projects in their own way. If you want to complain of what they do, you have to argue that they are incompetent or that they are crooked. Nobody has suggested that they are incompetent. But it has been insinuated that in return for money from the Fund they will oblige by digging up facts to support any prejudice that any officer or director of the Fund may have. This insinuation is so outrageous that it must arise out of acute alarm on the part of those who make it. What are they afraid of? I can only conclude that they are afraid of the truth.

Consider the excitement displayed in some quarters about the work the Fund has financed on the loyalty-security programs. In the first place, it was natural that this apparatus, which is estimated to affect ten to twelve million people, should attract the attention of an organization concerned with freedom and civil rights. Everybody knows that freedom and civil rights are restricted by the loyalty-security system. The American Legion Magazine bitterly attacked the injustices in the system in January 1955. For many months appeals have gone up for some kind of a public or private investigation that might discover the precise facts and lead to recommendations for action. As a result the Humphrey-Stennis Resolution, calling for a bi-partisan commission on the subject, passed both houses of Congress by almost unanimous votes and was signed by the President.

In the second place, the organization that has received money from the Fund to study the loyalty-security system is one of unimpeachable competence and integrity, the Association of the Bar of the City of New York. On the committee that it has chosen are leading lawyers of New York, Chicago, Washington, New Orleans, and Los Angeles. The staff director is a distinguished professor of law at Columbia University. The Association, like all the other grantees of the Fund, has absolute independence in conducting its study.

This brings me, in the third place, to the collection of cases made at the expense of the Fund under the direction of Adam Yarmolinsky of the District of Columbia Bar. Fifty of these episodes in the operation of the loyalty-security program have been published and have attracted a good deal of attention. Mr. Yarmolinsky has been careful to state that he has obtained the official records and all the other information he has published from counsel for the defense. He has also made it clear that what he has published is a random sample of the cases that counsel were willing to have published. Since Mr. Yarmolinsky dealt with fewer than four hundred cases, and since there are thousands of them, it was evident that Mr. Yarmolinsky's collection was not, could not be, and did not purport to be a comprehensive study of the operations of the loyalty-security program. It purported to be just what it was: a presentation of fifty cases on the basis of material supplied by one side. But what this material adds up to is the entire public record of each case. It is presented factually, without comments or recommendations.

One object of Mr. Yarmolinsky's work was to obtain data that might expedite the study of the Association of the Bar of the City of New York or any other that might be made of the loyalty-security system. Another object was to shed light on the importance or lack of it, as the case might be, of a comprehensive investigation such as that to be undertaken by the bi-partisan commission under the Humphrey-Stennis Resolution and that now being conducted by the Association of the Bar. The Yarmolinsky cases raise a presumption that gross injustice has at least occasionally been done in the execution of the presidential orders in this field. Since this is so, a comprehensive investigation is urgent. It ought not to be necessary for me to add that if the Yarmolinsky cases had raised the presumption that the system was operating perfectly, the Fund would have published them just the same, and would have done so with great relief.

I can only conclude that those who fear impartial investigation of the loyalty-security programs do so because they are afraid of the truth. The positions they have taken and the reputations they have built are interwoven with those programs. As John Lord O'Brian says in his book, *National Security and Individual Freedom,* "The great misfortune is that issues of loyalty and security have been seized upon by unscrupulous politicians and used as political weapons by selfish partisans." Such people do not want the system looked into, because they fear that it may be found defective, and their attitudes and reputations may appear defective, too.

It may be said that the Fund has a point of view. Of course it has. It believes that the principles of the Declaration of Independence and the Constitution are important. It believes that Communism and the methods of dealing with it are important. It believes that academic freedom, the protection of the rights of minorities, censorship, boycotting and blacklisting by private groups, guilt by association, and due process and the equal protection of the laws are important. The Fund believes that the facts about these issues should be brought to light and that the facts and the issues should be discussed.

I will go further. The Fund is for the principles of the Declaration of Independence and the Constitution. It is against Communism. It is for methods of dealing with Communism that safeguard the principles of the Declaration of Independence and the Constitution. It is against censorship, boycotting and blacklisting by private groups, and against guilt by association. It is for academic freedom, the protection of the rights of minorities, and due process and the equal protection of the laws. The Fund is perfectly aware that a tax-exempt organization must not seek to influence legislation, and it does not attempt to do so. The Fund has confidence that if the American people know the facts and understand the issues they will reach conclusions compatible with the principles of the Declaration of Independence and the Constitution. To quote the final words of Mr. O'Brian's book, "The public, with the issues clarified, will . . . respond to the sense of moral responsibility, and out of the present confusion will come a rededication to the cause of freedom in our time. In this confident belief must be our hope."

The point of view of the Fund for the Republic is conservative. It wants to conserve the Republic by conserving its essential attributes, which are freedom and justice. These ideas and the constant struggle to realize them in daily life have made our country strong and great. These ideas rest on a conception of man. According to that conception the ideal man is one who is willing to learn, but who thinks for himself; who respects the convictions of others, but who will stand up for his own against any power whatever.

In this country we do not have to take anybody's word for anything. The citizen does not have to take the word of diplomats about foreign policy, of military men about military power, of policemen about security, of informers about the disloyalty of persons, or of the Attorney-General about that of organizations. He does not have to take the word of legislative committees about the prevalence of witches. Though he is supposed to take the word of the Supreme Court about what the law is, he does not have to stop trying to get it to change its mind; and in America we recognize the claims of a higher law. We have only to recall Thoreau to be reminded that civil disobedience has a long and honorable history in this country.

Our reliance is upon the intelligence and character of the independent individual. The greatest dangers to the ideals that we cherish are fear and conformity. Courage and independence are the best guarantees of freedom and justice. We cannot feel free and feel frightened. The motto of the Fund for the Republic is "feel free."

THREE

THE FUND AND FREEDOM

The possibility of creating an independent corporation to discharge the obligation that the Ford Foundation had assumed for the defense of civil liberties was discussed among the Officers of the Foundation as early as August, 1952. The discussion continued among the Officers and the Trustees until February, 1953. The Fund was incorporated in December, 1952; but it was uncertain whether or not the total grant of $15,000,000 would be made until the Board of the Foundation voted it in February, 1953.

The Officers and Trustees of the Foundation, and the Directors of the Fund when they were elected, were aware of the dangers that a pioneering venture in philanthropy, and in civil liberties, would encounter. Senator McCarthy's star was in the ascendancy. The Cold War was raging; so was the Korean War. The Directors of the Fund were warned when they were invited to serve that their motives and actions would be misinterpreted. The Board had been carefully selected—each member of it was formally approved by each member of the Board of Trustees of the Foundation— with a view to indicating that conservative, responsible, distinguished people could and should be dedicated to civil liberties. But it was expected that efforts would be made to show that they were radical and irresponsible and that their reputations were unwarranted. This expectation was soon justified.

The first grant of the Fund was made to the American Bar Fund at the request of the Committee of the American Bar Association on National Security and Individual Rights. The Committee decided to study congressional investigations. Congressman B. Carroll Reece then charged that the Fund had been set up to investigate congressional investigations and deprecated the expenditure of $15,000,000 for this purpose. The total cost of the Bar Association's study was, as I remember it, something like $16,000.

Relative calm reigned, however, until the publication of the Fund's first annual report, which occurred in August, 1955. This showed that a group of eminent citizens was going to put a considerable sum of money into work connected with civil liberties and that they meant business. Immediately a campaign of denigration began, designed to discredit in advance the studies the Fund had announced and any others it might undertake. The charges ranged from the accusation that the Fund was undermining the national security to the remarkable suggestions that it was trying to prevent the renomination of the Vice-president and was in favor of granting a parole to the convicted atomic spy, Greenglass. These suggestions entitle those who made them to high rank among the imaginative writers of our time.

What the Fund is and what it does are things easy to understand. The Fund is a foundation seeking to defend and advance the principles of the Declaration of Independence and the Constitution. The methods by which it does this are studies, reports, and popular education. The studies and reports are designed to show what the facts are with regard to some alleged success or failure in the field of civil liberties. The program of popular education is designed to remind the people of their civil liberties and to bring to their attention the state of those liberties today. The studies and reports are made by the best qualified persons or organizations that the Fund can find. All that the Fund does is to decide on the problem, the individual or group that should make the study, and the amount of money that should go into it. The Fund has never at any time indicated to any one conducting any investigation any desire to influence its content or conclusions in any way. The Fund can be attacked for thinking that a problem deserves study when it does not or for selecting unqualified persons or organizations. Such accusations, however, are seldom if ever made. The Fund is attacked because of the conclusions reached by those in charge of the study or because of the conclusions it is feared they may reach. The Fund expressly stipulates, with those in charge of investigations financed by it, that it will not seek to control their results.

Many of the projects of the Fund make no recommendations. They are reports of the facts. The book by John Cogley on blacklisting in the entertainment industry is an account of this practice in this industry. It is up to the industry and the American people to decide whether they want to do anything about it. The report by Adam Yarmolinsky on cases under the Federal loyalty-security program was a statement of what happened to some accused persons. The report reached no conclusions and made no recommendations. The study by Paul Lazarsfeld and Louis Harris of anxiety among teachers will report the sentiments, whatever they are, of the teachers interviewed. The American people will have to decide, without advice from the authors, whether they think it a good thing for the country for teachers to feel as they do.

Where recommendations are made, they are those of distinguished citizens or organizations, not those of the Fund. The report of the Committee of the Association of the Bar of the City of New York on the Federal loyalty-security program will, if it reflects the views of the Fund, do so only accidentally. The Committee and the Association will arrive at their proposals without consultation with the Fund. The report of the Commission on Race and Housing will be unaffected by the fact that the Commission was financed by the Fund. A glance at the list of members will satisfy the most suspicious critic that even if the Fund wanted to influence the result, which it does not, it could not hope to do so.

In the field of popular education the promotion of discussion has been the rule. Here again the Fund has not sought to determine what should be discussed or what conclusions the discussions should lead to. It has made grants to groups that wanted to talk about civil liberties in a serious way. Its principal beneficiaries have been the Carrie Chapman Catt Memorial Fund, which carried on its Freedom Agenda program in more than 600 communities; churches and other religious organizations; bar associations; and the Illinois Department of the American Legion. The program of the Illinois Department is now spreading, without assistance from the Fund, to Florida and Indiana.

When distributing books or other materials the Fund is called on to exercise a judgment about whether one book is more worth reading than another, and there will always be differences of opinion on subjects of this kind. In general, the Fund does not distribute material that would be widely circulated without its aid; and it does not abstain from distributing materials with which Officers or Trustees may disagree. The criteria that it tries to apply are the seriousness and responsibility of the author, the timeliness and point of what he has to say, and the importance of getting the book into the hands of a larger audience than it might otherwise reach. In this type of activity the Fund cannot hope to satisfy everybody.

On certain elementary aspects of civil liberties the Fund has taken a position. It has made awards to the YWCA at the University of California, Los Angeles, and the YMCA at the University of California, Berkeley, because of the open platform policies of these organizations. This means that the Fund is in favor of free speech. The Fund made an award to the Plymouth Meeting of Friends because it refused to yield to pressure to discharge an employee regarded by its Library Committee as qualified and loyal. This means that the Fund has regarded as unfortunate the numerous attempts by private groups to dislodge from their positions persons whom their employers regard as qualified and loyal. The Fund made an award to the town of Waverly, Iowa, in recognition of the noble efforts of the citizens to find adequate housing for a Negro captain and his family. This means that the Fund wanted to encourage communities to provide minorities with decent places to live and not to discriminate against them on account of their race or color. The application of the Fund for the Republic for tax exemption stated that it would seek to defend and advance the principles of the Declaration of Independence and the Constitution. It does not seem possible, even if it were desirable, to require that the Fund should have no views whatever about the meaning of any of these principles.

Nevertheless, the Fund has refrained, as I have said, in all but the most elementary cases, from taking a position. Even in the South, where the decision of the Supreme Court tells us clearly what the Constitution means with regard to segregated schools, the Fund has largely limited itself to promoting racial harmony and co-operation through the Southern Regional Council and the churches of all denominations and to providing, through the Southern Regional Council and the Vanderbilt University Law School, information about current conditions.

The Fund is an educational corporation and must proceed by educational means. It does not "fight" for or against things, except as a university might fight. A university fights Communism, for example, in the only way that is open to it, when it finds out all it can about Communism and makes the information available. The Fund in its first official statement said that it regarded Communism as a menace to civil liberties. It has sought to find out all about it and to make the information public. Since it was widely believed that some of the methods used to combat Communism were unsuccessful and infringed on personal liberty to no purpose, it was obviously the duty of the Fund to examine the operation of the various ways in which the Government and other agencies had fought Communism, with a view to discovering whether these efforts were correctly or incorrectly criticized. The Fund assumes that the American people want to know the facts and that they are willing to have the facts presented even if in the process some sacred cows lose some portion of their sanctity.

This will always be the result of education in any field. Enlightenment means that dark places, such as those in which the sacred cows are usually stabled, are illuminated. Things look different in the light.

It will be remembered that the Ford Foundation, in making in 1950 the statement that became the basis for the Fund for the Republic, referred to "persistent international tension." International tension has always had repercussions on civil liberties in this country. The same men who adopted the Bill of Rights passed the Alien and Sedition Acts in the same decade because of the consternation caused by the French Revolution, and the epithets "Jacobin" and "anti-anti-Jacobin" were as popular, and often as ill-founded, as "Communist" and "anti-anti-Communist" are today. We may reflect with some pride and pleasure that the Alien and Sedition Acts did not last long.

We are a volatile people, capable of swinging from the depths of apathy to the verge of hysteria and back again in a short time and without notice. At some times we appear to be sunk in impenetrable indifference; at others we are scared out of our wits. We have gone to both extremes in facing the greatest totalitarian power the world has ever seen, Soviet Russia and the nations and organizations allied with her.

I am opposed to Communism because it is a form of tyranny over the mind of man. It is a system that uses a pseudo-religion to cloak old-fashioned imperialist expansionism, that sanctions the lie as an instrument of policy, that is based on the proposition that it is right and proper for a few of the people to push the rest of the people around, and that denies the essential elements of the American idea, which are freedom and justice.

I do not underestimate the threat of Communism; but I sometimes think that some people are so neurotically preoccupied with Communism that they underestimate America. Communism has failed in the United States. I hope I may not be thought unsophisticated when I say that it was bound to fail. When we know the facts and have time to think about them and discuss them, we are unlikely to lend ourselves to the support of any form of tyranny over the mind of man, at home or abroad.

The way to defeat an idea is to have a better idea. We have a better idea. The American idea is freedom and justice.

We cannot permit an enemy to use our dedication to freedom and justice in order to destroy them. We do not have to lay ourselves open to military attack, to espionage and sabotage, or to the operations of those who would change our form of government by unconstitutional means. But we might remember the words of J. Russell Wiggins of the Washington *Post and Times-Herald* to a congressional committee: he expressed the hope that "the time will never come when the situation in the world is so desperate that the only way we can prevent the Communists from destroying our free institutions will be to destroy them first ourselves."

Our success in combating Communism may depend on our ability to rally the rest of the world to our cause. It seems doubtful that this can be accomplished by military and economic aid alone. Such aid will also be forthcoming from the other side. What the other side cannot offer is freedom and justice. It cannot offer the American Dream, which has charmed the world for almost two hundred years. The decision of the Supreme Court holding segregation in the schools unconstitutional has done as much to reawaken faith in America as all the money and guns we have given other countries since the War. For the purpose of gaining the adherence of the peoples of the earth in the struggle with Communism the moral force of America is more important than her military and economic power.

The Fund has had confidence that if the American people had the facts before them they would respond by remedying those defects which diminish the moral force of America by lending color to the view that she is not as dedicated to freedom and justice as she claims. To some extent this confidence has been justified. The popular response to the Yarmolinsky report on the loyalty-security program and to the Watts report, also financed by the Fund, on discharges other than honorable in the armed services, was immediate and undoubtedly contributed to improvements in the procedures that the Government was using. The information disclosed offended the American spirit of fair play. The Stouffer report on attitudes toward Communists and radicals, which showed that many Americans are shockingly intolerant, not of the views of Communists, but of the views of all dissenters, probably did something to promote freedom of speech by arousing those who had not been aware of the extent to which that freedom was being suppressed. The forthcoming reports on blacklisting, race and housing, censorship by the Post-Office Department, and the intimidation of teachers are likely to have similar effects.

When the Fund was organized, it seemed important to awaken the interest of the public in civil liberties and to inform it about those situations in which the United States appeared to be falling short in practice of the ideals that it professed. The work of the Fund has approximated a survey of civil liberties today, together with a campaign of popular education. I think that this effort, which was essentially exploratory, was necessary, desirable, and, on the whole, successful.

In this effort little attempt was made to relate one study to another or to relate any studies to the clarification of important ideas. The guiding principle was found in the phrase "civil liberties" or in references to the Declaration of Independence and the Constitution.

The attack on problems as they have presented themselves, and the study of those problems in isolation from one another, have meant that the reports that have been issued and that are now in progress amount, of necessity, to commentaries on current events. Such commentaries, in the nature of the case, may not be very significant in time or space. As circumstances change, the relevance of investigations of the circumstances changes. A local problem may not have much meaning in another locality.

When the standard is urgency, there are many defensible opinions about what ought to be done. What is most urgent in terms of civil liberties or of the Declaration and the Constitution is likely to be decided on somewhat emotional grounds. It may be that the misunderstanding that has greeted some actions of the Fund has resulted from the lack of clear relation between the action performed and an idea that is widely understood.

A remarkable characteristic of the Declaration and the

Constitution is that they have been able to appeal to persons of different religious faiths, philosophical positions, and races and traditions. Everybody says he is for these documents. The critics of the Fund say so. The Fund replies that it is misunderstood. It seems at least possible that the Declaration and the Constitution are misunderstood, or are differently understood, sometimes so seriously that grave clashes can occur between proponents of different interpretations.

It is vital to demonstrate, if it can be done, that no matter what the ideas or background of the citizen, he can and must be dedicated to the principles of the Declaration of Independence and the Constitution. The Fund has not done much to clarify these principles. It has for the most part assumed that everybody understood civil liberties and was in favor of them. It has supposed that the disclosure of failures would result in efforts to remedy them. It may not have reckoned sufficiently with the proposition that in the present disorder one man's failure can be another man's success.

This is not to say that the effort to disclose obvious failures and celebrate obvious successes has not been in vain. This effort and elementary popular education should be part of any future program. The disclosure of obvious failures can prevent the Fund from retreating from the firing line; and rudimentary popular education can communicate the essential information without which no citizen can have any useful opinion about freedom.

We cannot, however, fail to notice the growing uneasiness in the West that results from the feeling that it lacks ideas, or an Idea, or at least a method of communicating to the rest of the world what its ideas are. For instance, on April 10, 1956, Dr. A. J. M. van Dal of The Hague, Secretary-general of the International Commission of Jurists, called for "a simple set of fundamental principles expressing in a readily understandable way the common denominator of our legal-political beliefs." He said leaders of the democracies lacked definite purpose and clear conceptions of what they stood for. Consequently, he added, the masses do not believe in any deep-rooted ideal. He said this situation often resulted in "too much improvising, too much taking a stand on incidental issues, too much changing of ground, too much confusion, disagreement, and disappointment."

With the rest of the world looking for leadership to the United States, we have not been able to make striking contributions on any but the economic and military levels. Ideas and ideals that we suppose were clear to our ancestors have tended to become forms of words useful as rhetorical flourishes or political weapons but without much visible effect in our daily lives. When we are asked what we stand for, our reply is likely to sound like a cliché or a slogan.

We have been busy with other things. The conquest of a continent, the great industrial and scientific development since the Civil War, and the changes wrought by two world wars have absorbed our attention, and our success has made it seem unnecessary to expend much energy in trying to figure out what we mean. Now that we stand at the head of what is called "the free world", we are called upon to explain ourselves. This is an indispensable step in holding the free world together and in attracting adherents to it.

It may be that the underlying problem of the Fund for the Republic, of the United States, and of the West is the same. References to freedom, justice, civil liberties, and the Bill of Rights may be inadequate to convey a meaning sufficiently precise and inspiring to arouse or maintain the devotion of the masses or to guide the policies of their leaders.

In order to avoid the slightest possibility of misunderstanding, I want to reiterate that I am not suggesting that only the adherents of one tradition or one philosophy can be dedicated to freedom, justice, civil liberties, and the Bill of Rights. On the contrary, my suggestion is just the opposite: it is that what is needed is a program showing that all men everywhere, no matter what their basic commitments to a religion, philosophy, or point of view, can and should be devoted to freedom and justice. A program that amounted to propaganda for one philosophical position would defeat, rather than advance, the attempt to reach "the common denominator of our legal-political beliefs."

What may be needed to give the studies sponsored by the

Fund greater permanence and universality, to develop a basis of common conviction in the West, and to show a pluralistic society how it can reach unanimous devotion to justice and freedom, is an attempt to work out fundamental concepts, and to make such studies, investigations, and reports as might assist in that endeavor.

If we want to make the Bill of Rights a living document today, we might ask what needs to be done to make it live. The tremendous growth of governmental activity and power suggests the possibility that new life might be injected into the Bill of Rights by a careful examination of its adequacy to protect the citizen today.

Nor is the change in governmental activity and power the only significant one. Maintaining the freedom of the press in an age of electronics, films, and enormous costs, is a different and more complex matter than it was when the press was made up of newspapers that could be run off by anybody who had access to a printing shop.

Or think of the change in the effectiveness of the drive toward conformity and the social and economic penalties it carries with it. This kind of pressure undoubtedly bore down hard on the inhabitants of the thirteen original states; but the history of the internal migrations of the period shows that non-conformists had an escape that is not readily available today: they could go from one atmosphere to another by the simple expedient of moving away.

I believe that the first three years of the Fund's work has been valuable. The Fund has stirred up interest in civil liberties; it has produced some changes in the public attitude toward them and has contributed to improvements in public policy. In the light of what it was supposed to do and of the circumstances of the time, the Fund properly started as it did. I personally feel the lack of the analysis and construction that might result from an attempt to work out the concepts basic to justice and freedom.

One result of such an attempt might be to clear up the confusion that is referred to in the speeches in the preceding section. I believe that most of the critics of the foundations and the Fund for the Republic are essentially devoted to the principles, as they understand them, of the Declaration of Independence and the Constitution. They do not seem to me to understand them very well, and they do not increase the clarity of their discussion by their careless distortions of simple facts and statements. But even if their motives were uncolored by political considerations, I believe that they would still, though devoted to what they believe are justice and freedom, disagree violently with many equally devoted citizens of this country about the meaning and application of these ideas. Discussion and criticism are essential to our society. But useful discussion and criticism can take place only in the framework of common principles commonly understood.

April, 1956

EPILOGUE

EPILOGUE

EPILOGUE

"Soviet diplomacy has faced the West with a tremendous and novel challenge. The West can choose to go on with the cold war. In that case, it must accept the consequent economic strain, and more diplomatic reverses of the kind that have pushed western colonialism out of Asia, are breaking up its position in the Middle East and tomorrow may begin to drive it from Africa. Or, on the other hand, the western powers can begin to disarm—and thereby face a different set of problems. Disarmament will not merely raise short-run questions of reconversion: it will raise the classic question of how capitalism can dispose of its surplus, and how it can find suitable markets. If they do not make—and export—guns, capitalist powers must make and export tractors, hydro-equipment and ploughshares. Then, directly in a large part of the world, they are led into competition with the Soviet system; and they have to compete willy-nilly. It is on this Leninist paradox that the new Soviet policy is founded. At this stage of world history, peace may prove a much more powerful social catalyst than war.

"If this analysis is correct, we cannot meet this challenge without a revision of policy at least as far-reaching as that which has been going on in Moscow. We, too, must bring ourselves up to date, for the policies that did duty in the cold war are totally inadequate for a period of competitive co-existence. Without a plan for diverting our resources to peaceful rather than stagnant military objectives, for changing our own economies and transforming those of the colonial world, the capitalist democracies will be impaled. What Marshal Bulganin and Mr. Khrushchev are asking us, however politely, is whether we will take the risk of making peace with them. What we must ask is how we can best equip ourselves to accept that risk."

These are the words of an anonymous writer in a British magazine that appeared April 21, 1956. I have quoted them at length because they have the ring of true prophecy. And not alone for that reason. The last two sentences seem to me to sum up the contradictions, the confusions, and the problems of our time. Imagine asking whether a country can take the risk of peace! We are used to thinking of the risk of war. We have grown accustomed to the risk of subversion. But the risk of peace and of peaceful competition—what can it mean? And when we ask how we can best equip ourselves to accept such a risk, what a dreadful confession is implied! Our splendid tradition, our elaborate educational system, our vaunted Way of Life are supposed to be the automatic answer to all questions. It is true that when we go to war, or when we have to deal with attempts to overthrow the government by force and violence, we are a little at sea, and we don't mind admitting that such occasions fit uneasily into our scheme of things, for we are a peaceful and law-abiding people, and proud of it. But to be thrown off our balance because a few men in the Kremlin have suddenly decided to make peace instead of war, to have to admit that we are at a loss to know how to deal with a situation that was normal for us forty years ago, this comes close to a confession of political bankruptcy. It is at bottom, of course, a confession of intellectual bankruptcy.

Our educational system ought to have some relation to our real problems, which are how to live in peace and how to make democracy work. Nobody knows whether either can be done. But everybody expected that the United States would show that both could be. And we have often seemed to be on the way to an effective demonstration of our ability to accomplish both objectives. We have, on at least two occasions, taken the leadership in organizing the world for peace; and we have come close to meeting, through the establishment of justice and freedom, the intrinsic difficulty of democracy, which is the protection of dissenters and minorities against the majority.

An educational system cannot promote peace and democracy by courses in Elementary, Intermediate, and Advanced Peace, or in Democracy I, II, and III. The great underlying illusion of American education is that if we have a need all we have to do is to introduce a course in how to meet it. This is why the weirdest reading available in the United States today is the catalogues of our colleges and universities, with all those entries about how to get married, how to get a job, and how to attain peace of mind.

The fact is that education accomplishes its purpose indirectly. An educational system cannot efficiently teach people how to do things, and, if it could, it would not be worthwhile, because of the high rate of obsolescence of such teaching. What an educational system can accomplish is this: it can produce the kind of people who can and will do the things that ought to be done. It can help the rising generation to understand what an important problem is; it can equip them with the standards and the disciplines they need to face such a problem, no matter what it turns out to be or what the conditions are under which it makes its appearance.

I do not despair of the eventual appearance of such an education in this country. But in order to achieve it we shall have to set our faces resolutely against the continuation of the triviality, mediocrity, futility, and irrelevance that now overwhelm our schools, colleges, and universities. This requires another and more constructive effort, the effort to make sure that we know what our important problems are. The knowledge of our primary needs is central if we are not to be carried away from time to time by assertions that what is actually needed are more engineers, or teachers, or nurses, or policemen, or whatever it is that people think are their needs of the moment.

An educational system that is worthy of the name is in effect a country's attempt to lift itself by its own bootstraps. The country has to want to be lifted, and it has to grasp the fact that this is the purpose of the system. This is the basis of academic freedom: the purpose of the system cannot be accomplished without the freedom to criticize. The country has to determine to put its reliance on the maximum development of its total intellectual power, which is arrived at by the fullest intellectual development of every person who composes it.

The trouble is that education takes time, and with hydrogen bombs, inter-continental ballistic missiles, superjet planes, and what not hovering over us, it is hard to settle down to the long, patient task that is education. It is hard, and it may be futile; for the rising generation may not have a chance to rise. The education of adults, which is in many fields the only valid education anyway, is now something more than a desirable activity designed to save us from the mounting boredom induced by our increasing leisure. Adult education, on a scale we have never dreamed of, is now an urgent necessity.

Because of the conditions of the media of mass communications, we suffer from an absence of organs of debate. Because of the condition of our universities, we suffer from the absence of intellectual centers. If some great foundation wanted to preserve and develop our civilization, it might consider establishing a model debating society in which a selected group of leading citizens formally argued, on radio and television, month after month, the most pressing questions before the country. Such a foundation might also give some thought to methods of bringing into being centers of intellectual illumination. This is what universities are supposed to be; but most American universities have abdicated this responsibility, and the rest, because of the confusion of their aims and the multiplicity of their undertakings, find it hard to discharge it.

Justice and freedom; discussion and criticism; intelligence and character—these are the indispensable ingredients of the democratic state. We can be rich and powerful without them. But not for long.

Gibbon opens his great work by saying: "In the second century of the Christian era, the Empire of Rome comprehended the fairest part of the earth, and the most civilized portion of mankind." The rest is decline and fall.

April 30, 1956

NOTES

MORALS, RELIGION, AND HIGHER EDUCATION

[1] "We must remember that the whole problem of intellectual education is controlled by lack of time. If Methuselah was not an educated man, it was his own fault or that of his teachers" (A. N. Whitehead, *The Aims of Education*, p. 96).

[2] Cf.: "All Souls College, Oxford, planned better than it knew when it limited the number of its undergraduates to four; four is exactly the right number for any college which is really intent on getting results" (Albert Jay Nock, *Memoirs of a Superfluous Man*, Vol. III, chap. 3).

[3] (London, 1939), IV, 193-94; also *ibid.*, p. 196.

[4] *Ibid.*, pp. 196-97; cf. Aldous Huxley, *Science, Liberty, and Peace* (New York, 1946), p. 9: "But in actual historical fact the spread of free compulsory education, and, along with it, the cheapening and acceleration of the older methods of printing, have almost everywhere been followed by an increase in the power of ruling oligarchies at the expense of the masses."

[5] There is some reason to believe that this is the group Milton had in mind when he referred to

". . . Eli's sons, who fill'd
With lust and violence the house of God."

(*Paradise Lost*, Book I, line 495).

[6] "Of new biological standpoints which last century gave us one most fruitful has been that of man as one of the animals. The thought is after all merely a return to the common-sense of Aristotle" (Sherrington, *Man on His Nature* [New York, 1939]).

[7] Cf. the report of O. H. Malik, vice-chancellor of the University of

the Punjab to the Preparatory Conference of University Representatives, published by UNESCO (Paris, 1948), pp. 132-33. "The main reason why Moslems wanted to divide the subcontinent of India was to establish a state in which they could live and work in accordance with the Islamic way of life. It is, therefore, natural that the Government of Pakistan has now decided that the educational system shall be inspired by Islamic ideology and shall, among other characteristics of Islam, emphasize the true Islamic principles of universal brotherhood, social justice and toleration. The universities have accepted this decision which, I believe, is one of the most important in the history of modern education. It does not mean, however, that the universities will be content only with instituting faculties of theology in which the principles of Islam will be taught and investigated. What it does mean is that the universities will endeavour to re-examine the entire field of knowledge, in so far as it affects, or is affected by, the Islamic religion. Its purpose is to assure that the student has full benefit of the Islamic point of view in his study of all the various branches of learning. He will, of course, be free to choose it or reject it, but it will be the duty of the universities to see that the Islamic point of view is not ignored. . . . I am conscious of the fact that the intellectual climate of today is averse to religion, at least in its revealed form, and that we in Pakistan are running a great risk of being regarded as mediaeval and reactionary because of our desire to integrate education and religion. . . . The differences of outlook between Islam and modern civilization are not over the scientific progress of man, but over the purposes of human life and the way in which such life should be lived if its ultimate purposes are to be achieved. A clear knowledge of these purposes of human life and of the ways and means for their realization is, according to the Islamic view, the finest goal of higher education. We regard education to be incomplete, or even dangerous, if it is not illumined by the spirit of religion."

[8] "I hear a great deal about character being the object of education. I take leave to believe that a man who cultivates his character consciously will cultivate nothing except what will make him intolerable to his fellow-men. . . . Character . . . is a by-product. It comes, whether you will or not, as a consequence of a life devoted to the nearest duty, and the place in which character would be cultivated, if it be a place of study, is a place where study is the object and character the result" (address before the Phi Beta Kappa Society, Yale University, 1908).

THE DEMOCRATIC DILEMMA

[1] This essay was written in 1951 when, it may be remembered, the fulminations of Senator McCarthy did what I said they did.

[2] I owe the discussion of this subject to the suggestions of Dr. Hans Elias.

[3] The reader is requested not to take the title of this chapter too seriously.

[4] I owe this discussion to the suggestions of Scott Buchanan.

SOME TRUTHS ABOUT THE FUND FOR THE REPUBLIC

[1] In addition to those mentioned as being on the Board of Directors of the Fund there were at the time of completion of this manuscript the following: Oscar Hammerstein II; Roger D. Lapham; and J. Howard Marshall, Vice-president, Signal Oil and Gas Co.

[2] Mr. Ashmore served from November, 1954 to November, 1955.

[3] Mr. Sherwood died in 1956.

Table of Sources

"Education and Independent Thought" was delivered in Santa Monica on February 20, 1952.

"The Administrator: Leader or Officeholder?" consists of two lectures. The first was delivered in a series at The University of Chicago on "The Works of the Mind" on April 23, 1946, and the second was delivered before the American College of Hospital Administrators on September 19, 1955.

PART III

"The Fund, Foundations, and the Reece Committee" was an address before the National Press Club on January 26, 1955.

"Some Truths about The Fund for the Republic" was an address before the American Veterans Committee in 1955.

"The Fund and Freedom" was written especially for this edition and completed in April, 1956.

"Epilogue" was written especially for this edition and completed in May, 1956.